Marlis Allendorf

Women in Socialist Society

English version by Ruth Michaelis-Jena and Patrick Murray, M.B.E.; F.S.A. (Scot)

International Publishers New York

Presentation   Volker Küster, Leipzig
Printed by Druckerei Fortschritt Erfurt
Library of Congress Cataloging in Publication Data
Allendorf, Marlies.
   Women in socialist society.

   Translation of Die Frau im Sozialismus.
   Bibliography: p. 215
   1. Women—Communist countries. 2. Feminism—History.
I. Title
HQ1588. A3713   301.41'2'091717   75–17597
ISBN 0-7178-0442-9
First U.S. and Canadian Edition 1976
by International Publishers Co. Inc.
Made in German Democratic Republic

Contents

*"I'll build houses—
pure dream houses. Quite different
from the ones we live in now.
My houses will bring people
together..."*

These words of a sixteen-year-old girl were in answer to a questionnaire circulated by a socialist magazine for youth, which had asked its young woman readers about their ideals for the year two thousand.

The words express the expectations and wide ambitions of a new young generation of women beginning life full of confidence, their imagination not clipped by the trammels of a workaday world. They are inspired by the determination to build a new world, the world of socialism.

Naturally, thousands of years of subjugation of women cannot be wiped out at one stroke, but with the new order of things under socialism a start has been made. Just as the exploitation of man by man is being overcome, so, too, woman will free herself from her ancient bondage. Then she can build houses full of grace and have dreams that will come true.

As woman marches away from her past, particularly that part which still shows so many traces of her degradation, she moves into a new world, one in which the old evil traditions no longer hold sway and nothing can choke her new femininity and dynamism. Freed from her former image she can now find her true identity.

This book attempts to follow and describe woman's path towards equality, often full of obstacles, yet joyous, for along it she has shaped her personality and enabled herself to play an increasingly effective part in the ferment of modern socialism; furthermore, the book attempts to make evident the relation between the individual and society, and the striving to achieve an equilibrium between the individual and his social environment. The development of woman in socialist society cannot be explained without taking into account history, background and tradition, since man is the product of his past. We must recognize the good and valuable things achieved before the advent of socialism. After all, the founders of scientific socialism, Karl Marx and Friedrich Engels, were raised in the schools of capitalist philosophy and economics. They studied everything from Aristotle to Hegel, sifting out whatever insights a fighting humanism of the past had contributed towards building a rational society.

Before presenting woman in socialist society we will therefore first explore the history of woman's liberation that begins with the earlier movement for emancipation in the eighteenth century, which is partly reflected in the ideas of the Enlightenment and passes into the larger movement for women's rights of the nineteenth century. It is doubly necessary to look at the historic roots as on the one hand capitalist so-

7

ciety has largely failed to recognize the law of historic development, and on the other, as a new class, the proletariat, has stepped onto the stage of world history in the nineteenth century only and has given new impetus to the fight of women for equality. In fact, from the nineteenth century onwards we are dealing with parallel and antagonistic forces in society which in their different ways have fought for a change in woman's position. The tension between these forces eventually gave rise to socialist theories and thought about woman's role, as seen in August Bebel's *Woman and Socialism*. With the fight of the working class for woman's liberation, matters moved from theory to practice and as the Russian Red October made theory into reality, so it allowed woman, as indeed all oppressed humanity, to move onto the stage of history.

Today millions of women live in the socialist society; and we have investigated the conditions under which they are achieving full stature. We have examined woman's education and training. We have looked at woman in her chosen career, in marriage and family. We have also looked at her charm, her femininity and tested her intellect and her emotions. Alongside the lofty and poetical aspects of woman's psyche, we have considered all the prosaic everyday circumstances, some of them remnants of the long, drawn-out process of emancipation, and we have looked at the need to overcome tradition-bound prejudice.

With all this we believe we shall provide something desirable and useful, adding yet another stone to the large edifice of writings about woman in widely differing times and places. We will supplement our world history of woman, consisting of many monographs, with the picture of a definite epoch. For the present this will be the final volume in the series.

Within *The Image of Woman*, published over a number of years, the present volume presents a type of human being socially "engaged" and no longer subject to a dualism of personal and public conscience. The image of woman in socialist society differs particularly from other social orders in that it is no longer necessary to call attention to particular outstanding women. In this society there are, next to the well-known faces, the many nameless women in town and country, in industry, science and art. They are all involved in their society. They are each unique, and their individual qualities are discernible to the observer. As the economic foundations of socialism eliminate the many distortions of the human image, and economic independence and social equality have afforded woman a new self-confidence, it appears legitimate to say that under socialism, woman, too, has attained a completely fresh human image.

This may be said for all socialist countries, and the present book is an attempt to illustrate our thesis.

The author, a sociologist and long associated with an important women's magazine, had to rely on the varying achievements of research in the different socialist countries, so that statements concerning individual problems are somewhat limited in their general applicability to the study of woman and socialism as a whole. It must also be remembered that national characteristics in the development of socialist countries affect—they may speed up or slow down—the pace of woman's emancipation. And it is because of this that the socialist countries of Asia and Cuba have been omitted in this study. The reason is not the geographical distance but their totally different traditions which would have to be investigated at length, to say nothing of having to consider as well the historical remnants of partial or fully complete colonial development.

However, we extend our greetings to those who have worked at their future with amazing energy and optimism, just as socialist Europe did, and who have led their women into a new world. It may be said with certainty that the experience and the knowledge collected here can be applied to all socialist countries irrespective of continent. What is dealt with is the inherent socialist society which, by its laws and economic and political structure, guarantees woman an all-enveloping chance of displaying her ability and talents.

We are concerned with these facts, assembled by a woman in the midst of socialist life who is close to the sources of most of her evidence. She herself spends her daily life in the German Democratic Republic, and it is obvious therefore that this republic must play a special part in the book, and quite naturally so since it provides an abundance of that detail which a study of this nature and subject demands. It was kept in mind by the writer that apart from scientific, or popular-scientific, treatment of the theme, art and literature have also felt the impact of the new womanhood. It is a mark of woman's achievement that her fellow citizens have erected memorials to women workers and artists, doctors, scientists and athletes.

The book's aim is also to encourage discussion about the image of Man in our time, to lead to new and fruitful consideration and at the same time relegate to the dust and silence of the upper shelf those outdated portrayals of woman which consider her only fit for the kitchen sink.

Our picture of women in socialist society realizes the vision of August Bebel, and the ideals of such socialist fighters as Rosa Luxemburg, Clara Zetkin, Nadezhda Krupskaya and many others. They fought for the rights of women and made real the vague dreams of humanist writers and thinkers and all those who have taken part in the bourgeois movement for women's rights.

We are here concerned with woman who is no longer in conflict with the world around her, but has gained her true place in it. A long fight and much sacrifice has been necessary to overcome the narrowness of woman's life in the past—forced upon her by the customs and ways of thought of so many nations—and to replace it by a great flowering of her special gifts and the realization of her true place. And a long road had to be travelled for the realization of all the poetic visions and revolutionary strivings.

Our century has achieved this in a large part of the world.

Dedicated to International Women's Year, our book presents WOMEN IN SOCIALIST SOCIETY as a contribution towards the image of woman in our time.

"I'll build houses, pure dream houses. They are meant to bring people together. They will be provided with communal domestic facilities, beautiful nurseries and playgrounds for all the children. And my houses will be serviceable, with movable walls ..."

Gundel

"Two thousand? My fiftieth birthday will be past. Funny thought: My children will then be grown up, and I will be a sought-after biologist of 'riper age'."

Marina

"By then I will have made it—long ago. I will be a woman expert in cybernetics. Cybernetics is the most interesting thing in the world. My husband, too, will work in cybernetics. We will both be professors at a university, or we may work in industry ..."

Karin

The dreams of these girls in the German Democratic Republic would have been the same in all socialist countries, and other young people would have answered questions in much the same way. Most girls have ideas about their future neither narrower nor more modest than those of boys. Their ideals are not more limited, nor is their imagination. They have the same self-confidence as boys. These are the daughters, in the Soviet Union even the granddaughters of women whose ways of life and thought were shaped by a stormy process, through years full of struggle and sacrifice. This process which changed man's condition is prosaically called the building of socialist society.

What a change has come about in life, in expectations, dreams and ideals, since scientific socialism inscribed on its banner the call to free all oppressed people, and with them to free woman. The call "Workers of the World Unite", which since the year 1848 has made the bourgeois world tremble, is directed at everyone oppressed, irrespective of sex. The small volume which first contained this call, and which, according to Lenin, is worth many volumes, namely The Communist Manifesto, is

"I will not have got used to the fact that there is no longer a winter anymore. In October an additional sun will have been shot into orbit over the northern half of the globe …"

Gudrun

"In the year two thousand I shall probably be a skilled worker in a factory which is completely automated. I will have a great knowledge of things, and can supervise production. So to speak: 'I will see through it all', even the most complicated processes. It is fun. I will know more than any engineer did in 1975. I will keep on learning because I want to. The level of pro-

duction will be so high that everybody only has to work for a few hours, thus leaving much time for my husband, my children, for all sorts of hobbies, and for learning …"

Gabriele

considered the birth certificate of scientific socialism. It is at the same time the first declaration of the emancipation of woman. But was woman then really able to take in the full meaning of this call, and follow it? Has she been able to, a being kept down for thousands of years, a slave before slaves were ever thought of? We have come a long way from woman's first awakening, from her first halt-ing steps at the side of the fighting oppressed, to the young socialists of today, and their dreams of the future. It seems an attractive undertaking now to trace back our steps from the present, an existing socialism, to test the reality, many layered, full of conflicts and breath-catchings, and so to discover the way by which history has confirmed the theories of Karl Marx and Friedrich Engels.

We will begin our investigation with a glance over the history of the fight for women's rights, a question which socialism does not consider a separate problem but part of the whole social question, something to be solved only in connection with the social revolution.

Dreams
Which Became
Reality

A Slave Forever?

The problem of the deliberate neglect and oppression of the female sex, and the quest for a way to end inequality, are much older than socialism. Apart from the many women who have rebelled against their position at different times and in different ways, the problem has occupied many great thinkers of past centuries. They have searched for the basis of the inequality of the sexes, and ways to abolish it. But too often, consideration has been given solely to the relationship of woman to her man and to the family, and only seldom to woman's position in society. The reason for this is surely that for centuries, right up to the time of modern capitalism, woman was not only subordinate to man, but was strictly limited in her sphere to home and children, with apparently little impact on society. How was woman cast for this part, this limitation to husband, home and child? Is this role natural and ordained by fate?

We can investigate this interesting question only in passing, in so far as it is allied to the relationship of woman and socialism.

The subordination of woman to the power of man can only be convincingly explained as the immediate result of the rise of private property. This is the view of many scholars.

In the early days of human society there was a period when women were equal to men, and even had a high standing in society. This was the time of matriarchy. The equal and at times superior position of woman in this period had two main reasons. First, woman played a great part in the development of agriculture, working with the digging-stick to feed the group. In this division of work, typical for early society, it was natural that woman, who at first only gathered herbs and vegetables, should in time become the farmer, while man continued the nomadic existence of the hunter. Woman became relatively settled before man did. The results of hunting were uncertain, but with increasing experience the results of tilling the soil became more predictable. Thus woman gained a temporary economic advantage over man which partly accounted for her place in early society. The other factor was the position woman held as mother in the group. The tie of monogamy did not exist, the father of a child could not be determined with certainty, and descent, kinship, could be traced only in the female line, from mother to mother. This produced economic independence, and matrilineal descent was the foundation for the early equality and social status of woman. Matriarchy came to an end when the further development of agriculture and the breeding of animals, founded on the hunt, demanded the greater bodily strength of man, and his experience with animals. Man became the owner of herds, and beneficiary of a growing trade in animals, skins, tools, and weapons. He now became the warrior who used prisoners as labor. For this new order of social life, ties to the group and matriarchal rights were a hindrance.

Riches in the hands of a single man brought him naturally into opposition to the primitive "communism" of the group, a system which enforced sharing and diminished the power of the individual. So the shackles of the old order which inhibited development were broken. Man detached the small family from the extended one, in order that his descendants might become his heirs. He made the soil – the most important factor in production – his own private property.

We do not know for certain the exact timing, duration and struggles of this revolution, yet it was one of the most decisive changes in the history of mankind. The change from matriarchy to patriarchy was not a simple historical change of positions. The overthrow of matriarchal rights was the historic defeat of the feminine sex. Engels wrote (1), "Man seized control of the home too, and woman became degraded and enslaved, slave of man's lust and mere means of procreation."

And it was August Bebel who formulated the often quoted opinion that woman, because of her economic dependence, was the first human being to become enslaved, that she actually became a slave long before slaves were thought of. (2)

"With the growing dominance of private property the subjection of woman to man was sealed. There followed the time of deliberate neglect, even contempt of woman. Matriarchal rights meant "communism", equality of everyone; the rise of patriarchal rights meant the dominance of private property, and at the same time oppression and enslavement of woman." (3)

When Friedrich Engels and August Bebel drew their readers' attention to matriarchy, it was not to picture this distant historic era as a golden age of freedom and equality, a lost paradise to be reconquered. The equality of primitive "communism" was equality of the sexes in an early stage of human civilization, equality in a very primitive way of life, and that freedom was far from real human freedom, namely the ability to shape one's life consciously, by free will, according to the laws of nature and of society.

Early woman was free from exploitation but was a prisoner of her ignorance, her superstition and simply her "primitiveness". All Engels and Bebel wanted to make clear to their readers, in citing the conditions of matriarchy, is the fact that subjection of woman to man is neither dictated by fate, nor a natural state, nor the result of the inborn cruelty of man. It is the direct result of the ascent of private property. Research in many disciplines has since established a more exact picture of all the related processes which have taken place over long periods and in stages varying widely in time and place. Definite matriarchal ideas can still be found in the early stages of class society, and, to some degree, they continued to influence woman's role in society, although this was also determined by her social standing in the class society. With the growing importance of private property went the steady and increasing decline of woman's rights relative to man. If law and the custom of Antiquity gave the slave owner the right to say: "Mine is the sovereignty of the house", the feudal lord had the might and right to declare that he was woman's warden and master, master also of all the wives and daughters of his subjects.

Because of her economic dependence and the might of her rulers who codified her dependence in laws, and sanctioned it by moral norms, woman throughout the centuries of which we possess written history was the main victim of oppression, exploitation, and violence.

Give Us Human Rights

Old as is the problem of woman's status, it only became a large and burning problem through the ascent of capitalism. The great changes which at the end of the eighteenth century brought final victory to the new mode of production, and particularly the French Revolution, with its call for freedom and equality for all peoples, led to the first conscious battle of large groups of women for their emancipation. It is beyond the limits of this book to go into the efforts of American women who—since the War of Independence (1774–1783)—fought intensely for their right to vote. But we will at least mention the fact that as early as the first half of the nineteenth century black and white American women had the courage to denounce slavery publicly. That was something extraordinarily new in history, and these courageous women exposed themselves to reprisals and persecution. When, for example, Angela Grimke held an anti-slavery meeting in Pennsylvania Hall, Philadelphia, in 1837, the hall was set on fire! Especially noteworthy is Harriet Tubman, the greatest American heroine of her age. "The General", as she was called, led over 60 slaves, including her entire family, out of slavery to freedom via the Underground Railroad.

The ideas of Rousseau and the Enlightenment, the general battle for emancipation from feudalism, had stirred the women of the rising bourgeoisie, and had prepared them intellectually for the onslaught against the old order. But louder than all ideas, the untenable economic conditions of a rotten feudal society spoke to masses of women, bringing misery to their families, unemployment, insecurity, and cruel exploitation.

In the Revolution, women of the lower middle class fought side by side on the barricades with proletarian women from the Paris suburbs. Their high spirits, their will to make sacrifices, and their courage have become part of the history of the Revolution. Théroigne de Méricourt, *l'Amazone de la Liberté*, was in the front line at the storming of the Bastille; Pauline Léon demanded from the representatives of the people arms for women and the establishment of a training camp. Unforgotten also is the Corps of Amazons, consisting of four thousand young French women, defying death.

Then there is Madame Lacombe, the actress, who was honored with the "Citizen's Crown" for her courage during the storming of the Tuileries. The beautiful and highly gifted Olympe de Gauges, too, is a remarkable figure of the Revolution. In 1791 she presented to the National Convention a declaration of the Rights of Women. In burning, passionate language she asked for full political and economic equality for women, as well as equality before the law. "If woman has the right to mount the guillotine", she wrote, "she must equally have the right to mount the speaker's platform."

This statement has become famous, not least because Olympe herself died under the guillotine. Her declaration like all other demands of the women of the Revolution, remained

March of the women
from Paris to Versailles, October 5, 1789.
Contemporary engraving

demands only. Clara Zetkin, the well-known German socialist, wrote about the outcome of this first great rebellion of women: "In spite of the sacrifices and the deeds of women, of masses of women, in the defence of the Revolution, human rights did not become the rights of women. Capitalism in its infancy had not yet affected a stable bourgeois society sufficiently to allow for this progress." (4)

Pre-Marxist utopian socialism could not advance the struggle for human rights and the equality of women, even though leading utopian socialists investigated the roots of inequality. Charles Fourier has the merit of having recognized, before Marx and Engels, and having formulated the concept that in any society the degree of woman's emancipation is a natural standard by which to measure emancipation as a whole. Solving the question of women's rights was connected even by the utopian socialists with the whole question of woman and socialism. But neither Saint-Simon, Fourier, nor any other critic of the existing order could point to a real solution of the problem. The means of production were as yet too undeveloped for utopian socialism to recognize the historical mission of the Common Man, and the link between the class-bound nature of society and the whole question of the status of women.

In Germany, too, the revolution of 1848 saw women on the barricades, fighting side by side with men for freedom. Among them were Emma Herwegh, Amalie von Struwe, Malwida von Meysenbug, and the founder of the women's movement in Germany, Luise Otto-Peters. They raised their voices for the equality of their sex, proving their energy and perseverance. But these women were few in numbers. They were not distinguished by independent actions, as were the women of the French Revolution. In later social-democratic writing it was maintained that those German "amazons" of 1848–49 put up more of a show than real action, and would hardly have used the daggers and pistols stuck so decoratively in their belts. But how could these women play a meaningful part in a completely ineffective and unfinished revolution?

However, that same revolution did become the cradle of the German women's movement. Luise Otto-Peters founded the first women's magazine, which bore the motto: "I call women citizens to the banner of freedom."

Nevertheless, this bourgeois movement had little effect on the masses of women, though some of these same bourgeois women strongly wanted to turn to their "poor sisters". Their love was not returned, because the difference in class was too obvious.

March of the weavers to Versailles,
October 5, 1789

Building a barricade. Paris, July 1830.
From a lithograph by Victor Adam

19

The shuttle flies
'cross the creaking loom,
We weave and we weave
through day and night—
We weave a shroud for Germany,

Into it we weave
a threefold curse,
We weave and we weave.

Heinrich Heine

Käthe Kollwitz. Tempest

Comfortable Home and Crowded Tenement

The life of women of all social strata was fundamentally changed by the dazzling development of industry, through the omnipotence of the machine and the vast concentration of wealth. As capitalism replaced man's labor with machines, so it made redundant labor which had been indispensable for centuries: labor in the household. The role of the housewife was fully justified as long as she, the most productive force in the family home, baked her own bread, spun, wove, dyed, sewed, even slaughtered animals and produced her own candles for light. But when machines started to produce all these things cheaper and better, the housewife's job gradually lost in importance, and the old-style housewife became, as early as the mid-nineteenth century, what she is now even to a greater degree—an economic anachronism.

Technical development literally snatched the housewife's work from her hands and drove her out of the house. An unrestrained technology destroyed the economic basis for woman's work in the family, but it created at the same time conditions and possibilities for her emancipation from kitchen and cooking pot. For this very development demanded her labor for thousands of activities in the outside world. Suddenly woman stepped into a world which until then had been man's domain. The destruction of what used to be woman's realm hit all classes and layers of society alike, although the rich were hit in a different way from the poor, and bourgeois women differently from those of the working class.

Women of the ruling class—once their spacious establishments no longer required the same amount of supervision—took time to enjoy life, played the "Lady Bountiful" to their less fortunate fellow-women, and some even contrived to educate themselves. Women and girls of the middle class, just to keep alive in the murderous struggle of competition, had to find a career which gave them a living should no suitable breadwinner turn up. For the majority of the women of the working class, however, heartless industrialism meant the dire necessity of selling their labor to industry. Either that or they saw their families perish since the income of their men was too small to feed an often large number of children. To these women the notion of "freedom to enter the world of man" seemed sheer mockery, for this very freedom meant nothing but a double burden for them: long working days in the factory and the care of the family as well, making their burdens heavier than those of centuries past. The very machines which ought to have brought greater ease to mankind and freedom from toil—which on the whole they did—multiplied the burden on the shoulders of working-class women.

The history of the machine is to a large extent the history of female labor. The machine took over the work of many hands and the two hands of an unskilled woman, in some cases even a child, could handle a machine. In that way the unskilled and cheapest labor was the most sought after by industrialists.

The consequence was mass unemployment of male workers, and almost incredible and increasing misery of the working-class family in Britain, France and Germany, in fact everywhere where the Industrial Revolution succeeded. Friedrich Engels in his book, *The Condition of the Working Class in England in 1844*, has dealt with much material documenting in a haunting way this very misery. Jérôme Adolphe Blanqui, a French revolutionary and utopian communist, speaks in his book on the French working class, *Les Classes Ouvrières en France*, of a worker's family in Lille where the husband in good times earned two francs a day, while his wife had to be content with ten to fifteen centimes. Even with the vastly increased value of the money of that period, this

The rising of the Silesian weavers,
Signal for the awakening
of the German working class.
Without plan or organization,
driven by despair and hate

for their oppressors, they gathered
their fellow sufferers, with women
their most determined allies,
to punish their tormentors.
Until the Prussian soldiers arrived . . .

still meant that their four children went out begging because the family, living on the most meager diet, could not afford the rent for their hovel, three meters below ground.

Between 1840 and 1860 such conditions were typical for many working-class families in Europe. Even after that time they were widespread, and for many life only became more bearable when the workers' movement gained some power, and the working class, influenced by the ideas of socialism, became aware of its strength as a class. Then the trade unions put up a fight to make industry pay a minimum-existence wage. In order to comprehend fully the situation of the working-class woman of that time, it is necessary to take into account the consequence of misery for family life. In the *Communist Manifesto* Marx and Engels had already attacked the sentimental bourgeois clichés about family, education and the loving relationship of parents and children. They pointed out that these very clichés were all the more distressing when all family ties were broken in a worker's family, where the children of that family were nothing but articles for sale and mere tools for labor. (5)

Working-class families lived under severe strain. Hunger, unemployment, dreadful slum conditions, illness, lack of education, alcohol—a cheap and yet far too dear method of drowning misery—the cares of a large family; none but the greatest love could conquer these. But, sadly, love, as is too well known, does need a base of material security! It needs at least the barest sufficiency of food and clothing if a family is to hang together, particularly in the case of large families. How then could there exist a common bond in direction, struggle and hopes between the woman of the wealthy class and the woman in a worker's family? The actual distance from the comfortable bourgeois woman's "doll's house" to the crowded tenement of her working-class sister may not be far, yet these neighbors are worlds apart.

Those bourgeois women interested in a change in society fought mainly for the emancipation of their own class in the everyday world. They fought for a place in the lecture-rooms of the universities, for the chance for women to be heads of schools, to be able, in short, to take their place in a more open society and to assume the same responsibilities as men.

The women of the working class, on the other hand, had to fight against an overload of work. Their fight, if it was to make sense, had to turn against the existing order of society, a matter which was never questioned by the bourgeois women's movement. Working-class women had to fight side by side with their men and not against them as did the women of the bourgeoisie.

It is therefore wrong to suppose that the socialist working women's movement arose, as far as organization and ideology are concerned, from the movement of bourgeois women.

There were, it is true, efforts by bourgeois women to expose the lot of women workers, to enforce improvements, and to draw the women of the submerged class towards the women's movement. Typical of these efforts was the women's movement in Germany which during the second half of the nineteenth century gained greater importance than in any other country.

Luise Otto-Peters was certainly outstanding among the fighters for women's rights, and from the very start she passionately defended the rights of women workers. Even before the revolution of 1848 she had written a novel, dealing with the revolt of the Silesian weavers, which proved her remarkable understanding, her courage and magnanimity. In the year of the revolution she wrote a passionate appeal to the ruling classes and to workers alike, to improve the conditions of women workers. Luise Otto-Peters believed herself to be a socialist. But her "socialism" sprang from the utopian faith that a system of reforms, and appeals to the humanity of the ruling classes, could basically change the situation. At the head of a movement founded by her, she fought against the excesses of Big Business, but not against capitalism itself, as an order of society, nor did she fight against the basis of this order, private property.

Chains of the Past

Women workers, suffering most severely from wage slavery, regarded the ideas of socialism as keys to open the door to a better world. The struggle of the growing social-democratic movement for shorter working hours, higher wages, protection for women and children, was a struggle for their very own interests. Unlike bourgeois women they were bound by neither property nor privileges to the existing order. What then would hinder them from questioning this whole order, including its basic assumptions about property and power, and from uniting with their male working-class partners to attack the root of social evil? Like her male partner, the woman worker had nothing to lose but her chains. On the contrary she stood to gain a whole new world.

Thus, as early as the first few decades of rapid industrial development there emerged a new type of woman in the working class. This woman, economically independent, and grown strong in the struggle against the thousands of life's adversities, had become a reliable, self-confident partner in the class struggle.

The number of women socialists, measured against the great mass of oppressed proletarian women, remained small in the beginning. A real movement of socialist women workers developed only in the early 1870's, at a time when the ideas of socialism had already conquered millions of organized male workers. The concept of woman and socialism, and a conscious movement of women workers, could become reality only when masses of working-class women recognized the true essence of the society in which they lived and suffered.

August Bebel maintained that a measure of insight and of freedom of movement is the pre-condition for man's entry into the socialist movement. Working-class women, however, were both in insight and in freedom of movement behind their male counterparts. Custom and education had narrowed their thinking and action and kept them from taking part in political education, and even more from entering into political activity. Their freedom of movement from childhood onward was restricted more than was men's by social prejudice and, above all, by the sheer weight of their domestic duties. A man's job was his only bondage, while women went through the same strain as men did at work and then after a long factory day had the full burden of domestic slavery, made all the more exhausting if they had many children. While the men attended meetings, obtaining information, read newspapers, and organized themselves, most working women had literally not a spare minute for relaxation, let alone the necessary energy for thought and thorough discussion. It is not to be wondered at, then, that originally women could not be easily organized.

August Bebel pointed to further reasons for the relatively late contribution of woman to socialism. Traditions which persist through generations, he said, become firmly ingrained habits and to men and women alike seem in the end natural and right, not to be questioned. (6) Clara Zetkin expressed this tellingly when she wrote that it was the "chains of the past" which weighed down the woman worker, and made her entry into politics more difficult. This also explains why the young and less inhibited women workers did not in the beginning tend to join the workers' organizations.

Young girls hoped for a marriage which would make life better for them than it had been for their mothers. They hoped for a husband who would at least provide enough to rescue them from wage slavery. Their work was not a life's career for them, but just a temporary solution until their marriage. They did not consider the trade unions an important matter except for their menfolk. The poorest and most exploited women were the hardest to organize. With minds blunted by misery they were not ready to spare even a few pennies for a worker's organization. These unorganized women also presented a much wanted labor reserve for the employer. Unorganized and docile, they took the places which their more militant sisters were often forced to leave. The greatest number of women to organize themselves worked in the big industries which employed masses of them, the textile and tobacco industries for example. It was much more difficult to reach the women employed in home industries, such as tailoring, and above all those in domestic service and agriculture. These women and girls worked on their own, and rarely came in contact with socialist ideas and political movements. In those days they had no contact with organized male labor, then the main carrier of socialist thought.

Where women were ready to fight side by side with men, reactionary association laws made their joining socialist organizations difficult. A whole number of laws forbade women in Germany and elsewhere from participating in any political association. "Womenfolk, pupils and apprentices", for example, were not allowed, according to an ancient Prussian law of association, to join such assemblies. "Such persons" also were not allowed "to take part in meetings where political subjects are discussed." One of the most important causes of the late entry of women workers into the political struggle, however, was that the socialist parties of all large industrial countries were not united as to their stand on female labor. As an example of this, Clara Zetkin speaks of a meeting of the social-democratic party in Berlin in 1866, which clearly demonstrated the confusion in the party over their attitude to the status of women. Their embarrassment, however, was overcome, according to Clara Zetkin, quoting in her turn Eduard Bernstein, by postponing the question of women's emancipation until the socialist state of the future had come into being, and condemning efforts to expand organized female labor as a prescription for providing a cheaper labor force to the employer. (7) What then should the workers' movements stand be concerning female labor? There was general uncertainty and workers' organizations in all industrialized countries were concerned.

Because of this the question was put on the agenda of the first Congress of International Workers' Organizations at Geneva in 1866. Karl Marx and Friedrich Engels were leaders of this congress. (8) The Proudhonists (9) demanded from the International that it should stand for the abolition of female labor. Woman's natural place, it was said, was the kitchen, and her natural calling motherhood. The Proudhonists and other middle-class socialists only saw the reactionary side of female labor, inseparable from uncontrolled industrialism, and quite overlooked its revolutionary possibilities. The Marxists stood for the right of woman to a career, stressing the connection between a career and economic independence. They saw in woman's independence an indispensable condition for her emancipation. The congress took a historical—the first—resolution on the question of equality for women, and at the same time demanded from the workers' organizations united in the International a promise to fight for better working conditions and protective laws for mothers and children.

The first volume of Karl Marx's major work, *Capital*, appeared one year after the congress. In it Marx again took up the subject of female labor, describing the devastating consequences of the brutal exploitation of women and children, its destructive tendencies and general hostility to the working class. At the same time he pointed out the revolutionary importance of the inclusion of women in social production.

The working class in Britain in the eighteen-forties. Friedrich Engels described their miserable lot, speaking of women who were never young, of children whose sleep was driven off by beatings, so that their work should not be interrupted. But Engels did not see misery only when he wrote: "Through their numbers alone this class has become the mightiest in England, and woe to the English rich when the workers become conscious of their power..."

Marx said, as vividly described by Clara Zetkin in her history of the proletarian women's movement, that as woman bore her cross in the factory, fighting courageously against great odds, she became the mason helping to build a new society. Careers for women, thought Marx, would be the future economic foundation for a higher form of the family and relationship of the sexes. This way of thinking gave the struggle of the workers for the liberation of woman a new theoretical basis, and, through the resolution of the International, a clear directive for solving the problem of women's labor. Women were not to be driven back into the home, but with equal rights and duties were to become comrades-in-arms for the cause of socialism. The First International in short was open to everyone, without sex discrimination. As early as 1867 women of the English Union of Shoemakers joined, as did the silk-weavers of Lyons in 1869. (10)

In Germany, workers' educational associations, who now canvassed for women members everywhere, played a positive part in winning women for the political struggle. Many of these organizations, however, tended to encourage women to take part in the bourgeois women's movement. But by developing in working women self-confidence, social awareness, and the will to fight, they created important psychological conditions for the start of the socialist women's movement.

In 1869 the International Workingmen's Association was founded. This organization, based on the ideas of the First International, saw for the first time a large number of women fighting as equals, side by side with men, in the struggle against exploitation. (11)

The efforts of these women mark the beginning of an organized class movement of working-class women. It was, says Clara Zetkin, "like the swallow which, according to the proverb, does not make summer, but whose appearance, all the same, fills the heart with joy and confidence, because it announces the coming of spring." (12)

The Dawn

The resolution of the International Working-men's Association regarding the equality of woman had repercussions in the emergent consciousness of thousands of women in Britain, France and Germany. In Britain the number of female members of the trade unions took a sudden leap upwards, and in France eight thousand women silk-weavers of Lyons joined the International, giving ample proof of the growing political awareness of many women workers.

In the summer of 1869 these same silk-weavers had gone on strike, demanding from their employers two francs a day and a reduction in working hours from twelve to ten. With the help of the solidarity of the International these demands were met after four weeks of struggle. In that way thousands of French women experienced the satisfaction of a great political success through joint action. Such successes were greeted with enthusiasm by the working class and strengthened their growing belief that through this very joint action they could bring industry to a halt. Solidarity on an international scale increased. In July 1869 the women workers in the silk factories of Lyons wrote to the Central Executive of the International in London: "We, the undersigned, members of the strike committee of the Lyons silk-weavers, declare in our own name and in the names of the eight thousand members, belonging to the co-operative we represent, that we have joined the International."

Jenny Marx—once "the most beautiful girl in Trèves", a loving woman, smoothing out troubles, civilized, a cheerful hostess, enchanting the great of her day with her charm and her intellect. All this has been said of her many a time. But she was much more. Jenny was Karl Marx's companion during decades of his restless life, poor in earthly goods. At his side she suffered want and persecution, mourned for the death of three children who died prematurely, and yet she was the light, in a life full of struggle, for a man whose work changed the world. Jenny was Marx's collaborator, had a share in the fight of organizing the working class. In that way she became the first woman to join the ranks of the working class in their conscious struggle.

N. N. Zhukov. Heinrich Heine visiting Karl and Jenny Marx. 1844

THE PARIS COMMUNE

For the first time in history
Workers in power.
And among them—typically
for the elemental revolution—
many women.
They threw themselves on the cannons
of the National Guard,
they defended the barricades,
defying death,
and very many died
at the wall of the Père Lachaise,
mowed down like grass
by the mitrailleuses of the
bourgeoisie.
One name became a symbol
for all the women of the Commune
for heroism and sacrifice:
Louise Michel.

This world organization spread the ideas of socialism among women, and drew women workers and the wives of workers of the industrialized countries into the daily struggle of their menfolk. It taught them to aim beyond their own immediate needs.

When matters came to a head in France under Napoleon II, and a military dictatorship brutally suppressed the people, for example confronting striking women workers with mounted troops, the women workers of Lyons, with courage and self-confidence, issued a manifesto asking young men to refuse military service. These were the first rumblings of the revolutionary thunderstorm which was to explode frighteningly and magnificently in the Paris Commune. (13)

Clara Zetkin described the struggle of these French women: "For the first time in any country the working class seized power, with valor and with a strong fist. This powerful event did not lack the typical feature of any elemental revolution, namely the taking part in it of large numbers of women. It began on March 18th, 1871 when the women of Montmartre threw themselves bodily onto the guns of the National Guard to keep them from being taken to Versailles, and the women persisted to the very last struggles in that bloody May week when government troops mowed down the rebels like grass at the wall of the Père Lachaise cemetery. Women of the Paris working and lower middle class, fully recognizing their duty to the revolution, mounted guard, gave first aid to the wounded, and helped build and defend the barricades. The barricades in the Place Pigalle were held to the last by women, facing the enemy, disregarding

death, arms at the ready. An English reporter wrote admiringly and alarmed at the same time: 'If the French nation consisted of women only, what a terrible nation it would be'." (14)

One name among the fighters of the Commune has become a symbol: Louise Michel. A Paris teacher, she was a convinced revolutionary, a sensitive, intelligent woman who fought bravely in the ranks of the Communards. After the defeat Louise Michel was deported to New Caledonia, an island in Melanesia where many Communards perished under the torture of forced labor and fever. After nine endless-seeming years of exile, Louise Michel received an amnesty. Unbroken and deeply infused with socialist ideas, she took up again in France the fight against social misery and the oppression of the people. She was imprisoned several times, and her memoirs are a precious legacy of a life spent in the struggle for the betterment of mankind.

After the Paris Commune was brutally defeated in May 1871—thirty thousand men and women were shot, tens of thousands languished in prisons or labor camps—the center of the international socialist movement shifted from France to Germany. Marxism had taken root in the German working class which, possessing an advanced social-democratic movement, could build on the experiences of the British and French working class. The German working class, however, had to face a particularly reactionary and aggressive enemy in the Prussian-German military state. In spite of these circumstances, and in spite of brutal suppression, the social democrats became in the decades to follow one of the most esteemed and most powerful among the socialist parties

of the International. Organized women workers kept in step with these developments, well encouraged by men like August Bebel, Julius Motteler, and others. Soon they were to find in Clara Zetkin an excellent leader and teacher, and the movement of women workers in Germany became an example for the fight of socialist women in other countries.

In Germany, unlike in France, women were not confronted with socialist ideas in spectacular revolutionary events. Rather, they witnessed a process of gradual evolution taking place in the workers' movement itself, in often heated arguments about the whole question of working women. The influence of socialism on women's thinking was a turning point. "For the first time women became aware of the shortcomings of the established order, and began overcoming outmoded prejudices, putting new ideals into their place, re-thinking their own life and work." (15)

The trade unions, founded in 1869, were the true beginning of the relationship of women workers and scientific socialism. They had their main center in Saxony where the textile industry was then moving from home craft industry to industrial production. The decline of home industry was accompanied, particularly in the region of the Erzgebirge, by an impoverishment of the local population, comparable only to the misery created by the beginning of industrialization in Britain.

This economic development in the Saxony textile industry, and in particular the brutal exploitation of women and children, prepared the ground for the seeds of socialist ideas. A network of workers' associations began to spread throughout the country. These organizations no longer could or would dispense with the cooperation of women. According to Clara Zetkin: "The traditional views of the difference between the sexes, and of what is suitable for a woman and what is not, were defeated by the simple facts. Now the workers' associations recognized that women, too, were the slaves of industry, not essentially different from their male counterparts. And they were ready to be enrolled into the ranks of fighting socialism." (16)

The trade unions had become fighting organizations, and in the *Reichstag* August Bebel had passionately declared their strong sympathy with the fighters of the Paris Commune. Working men and women in Saxony had joined the courageous protest of all social democrats against the Franco-Prussian War of conquest. All this exposed the trade unions to drastic persecution by the new Prussian state, born of "blood and iron". In many places these organizations, their membership diminished by the war, were dissolved by the authorities. This, together with the economic crisis and starvation, drove many families of active workers to emigrate. Thousands began a new life in America. The decay of the trade union organizations could therefore not be avoided, but they had done much to prepare the ground for new forms of organization, and for the fight in spreading socialist ideas among the working class.

As far as women are concerned, suppression and persecution only served to tie them more closely to socialist ideas and the workers' movement. In 1872 in Berlin, an association of women workers was organized in close contact with the Marxist wing of the social democrats, in which, later on, Clara Zetkin was to play a leading part.

The most essential feature of the early women workers' movement in Germany was the widespread belief in the necessity of a common organization. This would consist of all workers without discrimination as to sex, honoring woman as a companion with equal rights and duties in the working-class struggle. Thus women would be clearly directed towards the aims of a socialist society.

A Book Changes Millions

As part of the repressive measures against German socialists after the chauvinist victory intoxication following the Franco-Prussian War, August Bebel was prosecuted for high treason and lèse-majesté. By then Bebel was already a prominent leader to whom even his political adversaries in the *Reichstag* listened with attention. He was a modest man without pretence who activated the masses, filled them with enthusiasm, and carried them along with him wherever he appeared. It was said of Bebel that he combined an intimate knowledge of the working class with quite outstanding ability.

He used well his three years of imprisonment at the fortresses of Hubertusburg and Königstein, and the Zwickau prison, and the book he had written during that period appeared in 1879. It seized hold of the whole progressive world, and remains a textbook for the international workers' movement to this very day. It became the most widely distributed product of socialist literature in the nineteenth century. The socialist women's movement regarded it as their book of books: *Woman and Socialism.*

The book was published in Switzerland because Bismarck's anti-socialist law for twelve years, from 1878 to 1890, suppressed rigorously the social-democratic press and all manifestations of socialism in Germany. The title of the book was simple and insignificant for a work of such magnitude and revolutionary impulse. Yet, at that time, and under the conditions of illegality, the mere linking of such concepts as "woman" and "socialism" carried so much ideological dynamite that Bebel changed the title to *Woman in the Past, Present, and Future*. Some copies even had an extra masking dust jacket bearing the legend: *Reports from the Works Managers*. A thousand ways were found to distribute Bebel's book illegally in Bismarck's *Reich*, mainly through the *Rote Feldpost*, as the social democrats proudly called their illegal book distribution scheme. It was the very suppression which made the book's fame. Everybody talked about it, if only in whispers. An article in the contemporary press stated that even wives of ministers of the crown and their daughters managed to get

hold of it, and from their reading perhaps learned to recognize their own undignified position in society. The reverberations of *Woman and Socialism* livened up the discussions about woman's status in all strata of society, mainly, of course, among organized labor. The more vigorously it was attacked and reviled by the enemies of socialism, the more the interest in it mounted. This great interest in and success of Bebel's book did not rest solely with his masterly writing nor with the spirit and passion with which he advocated an end to thousands of years of injustice. It was the subject itself, a subject which by now had become a daily problem in the workers' movement, a problem urgently calling for solution. Was it really possible for the workers' move-

ment, struggling under the yoke of the reactionary laws of a reactionary state, and gathering all its strength for the fight, to do without its female component, actually half of its members? In spite of all progress in the international trade unions, the workers' movement as such still harbored prejudices against the inclusion of women in the socialist movement. Now these prejudices, more than ever before, became obstacles, weakening the movement.

Bebel had already given much consideration to the place of woman in society earlier on. He, the son of a poor widow who just managed to scrape out a living for herself and her child, knew the life of working women. As a young revolutionary he had been an adviser to the women of Saxony, present in the *Internationale Gewerksgenossenschaft*. In his speeches in the *Reichstag*, and at hundreds of workers' meetings he never tired of attacking uncompromisingly the ideology of the natural inferiority of women. This ideology could only help the ruling classes in their fight against socialism. For the revolutionary worker, however, it meant the loss of an army of potential female comrades.

It is Bebel's merit to have made clear to millions of men and women the inevitable interrelationship of woman's status in society and the working of that society as a whole. Bebel treated questions concerning women as a historical-social process, while his bourgeois contemporaries approached the subject as a psychological problem related to "woman's nature". Bebel started firmly from a basis of scientific socialism, and this historical approach gave him, a self-educated wood turner, a point

of view much superior to that of the academic of his period. Bebel considered woman's past, present, and future, and from the very beginning drew a distinction between bourgeois and socialist concepts. Early in his work, after laying down his first basic principles, he wrote: "... It becomes quite clear after these arguments that, if this book were concerned only with showing the need for woman's full equality with man, socially and politically, on the basis of our present society, I had better not write it at all. For in that way a genuine solution to the question could never be found. A full solution of it ... is, under the present social and political institutions, as impossible as the solution of the workers' problems." (17)

Clearly, leaving no room for doubt, Bebel maintained that the liberation of woman can be made possible only under socialism. Therefore struggle for equality of the sexes must be struggle for socialism at one and the same time.

The first part of Bebel's book traced the unhappy path of woman through the different historical stages of exploitation which changed only the form of oppression. With a mass of authentic documentation and statistics he held up a mirror to the existing society, described the double exploitation and the absence of rights of the working-class woman, showing as a cause of all her misery the yearning of Big Business for profits only. The ruling classes were sorely hit by his criticism, in which he relentlessly laid bare the moral swamp created by the prevailing system. He lashed out at the double morality of so-called High Society, as expressed, for example, in marriages for

money or titles. With sarcasm he quoted a typical advertisement from a very patriotic Leipzig newspaper: "Officer of the *Garde Kavallerie*, tall, handsome appearance, old nobility, twenty-seven years old, wishes money match. Addresses please, poste-restante *Hauptpost*, Dresden, under Graf v. W. I. ..."

Bebel remarked that, compared to a man making that cynical offer, a prostitute plying her trade out of bitter need, would seem "a model of decency and virtue." (18)

Bebel demonstrated the class character of the state, talking righteously of democracy and justice and then using every means in its power to set its suppressive machine in motion when the working class tries to implement these very concepts.

All Bebel's research and disclosures were never used by him as ends in themselves or for cheap sensation. His one and only aim was to guide his readers firmly towards the one great recognition: the liberation of all oppressed people can only be achieved through socialism. There is no other way. Bebel's whole life was devoted to this cause. He was also a dreamer who could describe his dreams for the future in vivid language, and he cared nothing about those who mockingly called his work a "green Baedeker for the Land of Utopia". Whoever now reads Bebel's vision about woman in socialist society, and looks at things as they are, must realize that his ideas were by no means utopian, but founded on realistic foresight. "... Woman in the new society," he wrote, "is socially and economically completely independent, not subject any longer to even the slightest exploitation. She is an equal of man, free and sole controller of her destiny. Her education

is the same as man's, taking into account differences of sex, and woman's special functions. Living under natural conditions she can develop and use her physical and intellectual strength and abilities according to her needs. She will choose for her work those fields which suit her wishes, inclinations and gifts, and will work under the same conditions as man. In the choice of a partner she is as free as a man. She will marry or get married for no other reason than affection and love." (19)

The recognition that the full emancipation of woman can be achieved only in a socialist society did not tempt Bebel to postpone the struggle for emancipation until this distant state of the future, even though there were at the time enough opportunists among German social democrats who would have been pleased with that sort of solution. Rather, Bebel called on women to fight here and now alongside their men for the victory of socialism. Woman, said Bebel, should be aware of her true role in the movement and in the struggle of the day for a better future, and be determined to take her part.

His book was taken by all concerned as a guide to action. Through it he helped directly, and indirectly by the impulse it provided, to raise the class consciousness of the oppressed and intimidated working-class woman. He strengthened her self-confidence and her readiness to flock to the banners of socialism. In that way Bebel was a pioneer in the development of the German and international revolutionary women's movement. At the same time the publication of *Woman and Socialism* ended a period of arguments in the German workers' movement concerning their stand

over woman's liberation. In 1910, writing in the women's paper, *Die Gleichheit*—Equality— Clara Zetkin clearly foresaw Bebel's importance for the German and international workers' movement. And her testimonial may stand here to honor a man to whom every progressive woman in the world owes much gratitude.

"Frail written pages may be scattered in the wind, but Bebel's memory will live, along with what he meant to the rising working class. His finest monument will be the achievements of the people whose will he helped to direct towards the mightiest deed in the history of mankind: the building of a new society." (20)

Max Liebermann.
Women Workers in a bottling factory. 1879

"To Fight Where Life Is…"

Up to 1890 all political activities of the German socialist movement were banned. Only the group of social democrats elected to the *Reichstag* could not be suppressed by Bismarck. When August Bebel and Wilhelm Liebknecht organized the underground movement, and the outlawed social democrats, after a period of confusion, found a thousand ways to continue the struggle, not only were they able to unite larger and larger numbers of workers under the red flag, but women were at their side. Untiring, skillful and full of ideas, they undertook the dangerous small tasks of the illegal fight. In the resistance against repression, solidarity grew between working men and women. Less and less credence was given to the opinion, still current in some parts, that because they were without political rights, and therefore without power, women were of no use in the struggle. Practice confirmed what Bebel had stressed again and again in his book, that if working women and the wives of workers were drawn into the socialist movement and made acquainted with its ideas and aims, they would become indispensable and determined participants. They proved excellent during the great strikes of the 1890's which in turn proved the strength of the working class in Germany and in the world at large. During the time of the German anti-socialist law masses of social-democratic workers were dismissed from their jobs. Many leading socialists were sent into exile, having to leave their families without protection or livelihood, and thousands of social democrats were put behind bars in the Prussian state. During this period of stress it was not least the wives of workers who again and again kept the lines of communication open. They warned those in danger, saw to it that books and papers reaching Germany from abroad arrived at their destination via the *Rote Feldpost*, to keep workers up to date with what was happening. They supported the families of the unemployed and exiled. Also, women knew as well as men that in times of oppression joy and diversion play a mobilizing role. So singing clubs sprang up, music lovers' and ramblers' associations were formed and informal get-togethers of workers, groups of small animal breeders and bee-keepers were organized. In the years of the anti-socialist law these were not only skillful cover-ups for the continued existence of the workers' party and the trade unions, but also greatly helped to create social activities hitherto unknown and unthinkable in the labor movement. They deepened the sense of solidarity of working-class families. Support from the leaders of the world proletariat, Bebel's wealth of ideas for organization, the great wave of strikes in all industrialized countries—all these contributed to the self-confidence and courage of the international movement. Eventually the discipline and steadfastness of men and women workers forced the repeal of Bismarck's special law. Victory over twelve years of oppression and persecution was a victory of solidarity in the widest sense. In 1889, strikes had reached their peak—5% of all German men and women workers were on strike—and in January 1890 the anti-socialist law collapsed.

The rise of the international socialist movement in Germany and indeed in all industrialized countries during the late 1880's, their broadening out, and the coming into being of large and powerful socialist parties, required a new stage of international cooperation.

At the congress in Paris in 1889 when the Second International was founded, a young woman mounted the speaker's platform and in an impressive speech, the first of her life, pleaded the cause of women. The young woman was Clara Zetkin whom we have mentioned before. Now thirty-two years old, she was to play a leading part in the international socialist women's movement. Born Clara Eissner, the daughter of a village teacher, she was brought up in Wiederau near Chemnitz, and herself became a teacher later on. In 1878 she passed her exams with distinction, but even though she was dedicated to her profession, and preoccupied for the rest of her life with questions of child education, her career took a turn different from the plans she had made for herself in her early youth. Before the anti-socialist law, and under the influence of the Russian revolutionary, Ossip Zetkin, who later became her husband, Clara had joined the social-democratic party in Leipzig. From that day onwards her life belonged to the fight for socialism. She took part in the illegal work of the party, and with her husband shared the hard fate of the emigrant. She was widowed when she was still quite young. So, when delivering her speech at the congress, Clara was young in years, but a socialist woman well-tried in the struggle. By then already her character had been shaped by her life's motto:

"To fight where life is." The speech at the Paris congress was not only her first big speech, it was actually the first time in history that a woman defended the right of equality for her own sex in front of an international gathering. She put the subject of *Woman and Socialism* on the agenda, scientifically precise and with burning passion. "While women," she said, "fight side by side with the socialist workers, they are ready to share all sacrifices and hardships, but they are also firmly resolved to take as their due after victory all the rights that belong to them." It is to Clara Zetkin's credit that the Second International set the pace for socialists of all countries to draw women into the class struggle.

When, a year later, the German socialist party formulated its new program, the Erfurt Program, it contained, true to the resolution of the International, the demand for woman's economic, political and legal equality. In the same year, after the repeal of the anti-socialist law, Clara Zetkin was able to return home with her two children. She became the co-founder and editor of *Die Gleichheit*, a women's paper which fought for the interests of the international socialist women's movement. She edited the paper for twenty-five years, and as a highly gifted publicist always kept her finger on the pulse of the time. Taking up the problems which most agitated women, she found the right tone to arouse popular awareness.

Meeting of Women Workers in Berlin, about 1890.
From a contemporary engraving

A WORKING-CLASS MOTHER
TALKING TO HER SONS
AT THE OUTBREAK OF WAR

Now that you go forth to do your
masters' bloody business,
the enemy's guns in front,
behind you the officer's pistol,
do not forget:
Your masters' defeat
is not yours. And neither is their
victory.

Bertolt Brecht

Fritz Junghanns. Woman with coffee grinder. 1931
Hans Baluschek. Working-class women. 1900

CLARA ZETKIN

The theme of her fulfilled life:
Woman's liberation and equality.
She knew Friedrich Engels,
and discussed things with him.
She was August Bebel's
valiant comrade,
fighting for her convictions
for quarter of a century
as editor of "Die Gleichheit".

And her motto:
"To fight where Life is."
Her finest hour came when she,
Clara Zetkin, as Lenin's close friend,
lived to see the victory
of the socialist revolution,
and well into old age could help
to change the ideal of equality
into living reality.

The first annual volumes of the paper give a vivid impression of the growth of the working women's movement, and of its stand concerning the important political and economic problems of the day. Every issue contains an article exposing the scandalous exploitation of women. There were, for example, the women workers in the jute spinning works in Bremen who earned 14–15 pfennigs per hour, many of whom could only treat themselves to one hot meal a week. For two to three marks a week young girls in Saxony took the fired china from the kiln. Because of the great heat, they could wear only a shirt at work, and were often exposed to draught, nearly all of them ending up with rheumatic complaints. Women sewing blouses lived far below the existence minimum. The layout of *Die Gleichheit* was modest, its contents geared to the struggle and well removed from the sentimentality of bourgeois publications. At times, however, and

Eugène Laermans. On the evening of the strike. 1894

true to the period, writing was emotional, for example: "It is not linen that you wear out, but warm human life . . ."

In Germany laws still prohibited the participation of women in men's associations. Because of this, "agitation committees" were formed which systematically and according to laid-down plans acquainted women with socialist ideas. In ever larger numbers working women joined the socialist women's movement. The agitation committees called public meetings where sometimes over a thousand women took part. They issued proclamations, and appeared at trade union meetings. At the same time educational associations for women and young girls were founded in all big cities. When, after the rejection of the military bill put forward by the government, the German *Reichstag* was dissolved in 1893 and new elections were prepared, thousands of women took part in the election campaign of the social-democratic party, even though they themselves were not allowed to vote. Women visited house after house, ran up and down stairs, collected money for the election funds, explained the aims of the party, carried posters through the streets, copied voter's lists, and gathered up dilatory voters on election day. With much gaiety the women of the socialist movement coined the phrase: *"Und können wir nicht wählen, so können wir doch wühlen"*—if we can't vote, we can at least agitate—the fun being in the German pun of *wählen* and *wühlen*. And the women went beyond working at mere details. They learned to organize and chair meetings and conferences. The summer of 1893 brought repressive measures and prohibition of the agitation committees and working wom-

en's educational associations. In some cities, Nuremberg and Altona for example, not only the executive committees, but the whole membership of these associations was dragged into court. However, the women now facing reactionary forces could no longer be compared to the humble oppressed females of the past. They had by now taken part in the illegal struggle against the anti-socialist law, had proved themselves in the massive strikes, contributed to the election victory of the social democrats, and they now defended courageously and confidently what they considered their rights. In Nuremberg, for example, when sentence was pronounced against active members of the working women's association, all the members—fifty-nine women—appealed. At the second hearing, made necessary by the appeal, the bewildered court faced a crowd of women; fifty-six of the fifty-nine members turned up, the three missing ones being ill at the time.

When the police drove women from meetings of the social democrats or trade unions, they listened to the speakers from nearby rooms or through open windows. Repressive measures only strengthened these women's will to fight, and it can justly be said that in the history of women's emancipation the years from 1893 to the turn of the century were the age of the working women's movement.

It was in these years also that the final division of struggle became clear between the bourgeois and working-class movement. Associations of bourgeois women were formed in large numbers in the 1890's. Some of them were conspicuous for the astonishing manner in which they fought against anything called "man", but that did not guide them into lifting

a finger when it came to helping the persecuted working women's associations. But it was not superficialities or the unwillingness of the bourgeois women to help their poorer sisters which led to the final and complete divorce of the two movements. Rather it was that the organized women workers had clearly recognized the gap in social awareness which could not be bridged. They recognized the basic difference between the movements to say nothing of their totally different aims.

The minutes of the meeting of the social-democratic party at Gotha in 1896 state: "... in spite of the many points of contact in legal and political demands for reform, the working-class woman has no common ground with the women of other classes, regarding the decisive economic interests. The emancipation of the working-class woman can therefore not be brought about by the women of all classes, but is solely the task of the working class irrespective of difference in sex."

The German working women's movement was the most important, and the one most closely connected with socialism. In other industrialized countries, too, the socialist women's movement increased in strength and numbers with the development of the worker's movement as a whole. In the program of all socialist parties the emancipation of women now took the place it deserved, last but not least due to the powerful responses among international workers to Bebel's book. Clara Zetkin's paper reports at this time conferences and actions by Austrian, British, Czech and Italian social-democratic women workers. An organization of social-democratic agricultural women workers was founded in Hungary.

A famous old picture
of the life of the people under
the tsarist yoke.
The painter is unknown,
as are the Russian women who,
like animals,
tow along a boat.
They must walk under the yoke,
and neither God nor Tsar
takes pity on them.
And little Mother Russia's love
is but meager for the oppressed.

It held a congress in 1898 which was attended by delegates from 250 places. These Hungarian women reported the growing socialist influence in the country, and demanded effective protection for female agricultural laborers and the right for women to vote.

In only few other countries, socialist women workers were hampered as much by the laws of association, by persecution and prohibitions as in the reactionary German *Reich*. This had forced them into organizations of their own. Where laws permitted, women in the industrialized countries were members—with equal rights—of the social-democratic parties. In Germany this was possible only after 1908. They then sat on committees where they could plead the cause of woman inside the parties. However, the many struggles and the persecution to which organized German women workers were exposed had their advantages also. They brought about the early and consistent collaboration of these very women with revolutionary social democracy.

The development of the socialist women's movement—now established in a number of countries—created the conditions for international cooperation which the women of Clara Zetkin's circle desired fervently. This collaboration became the more necessary, the more chauvinistic and aggressive the spirit of the period became everywhere. In Germany in particular, capitalism had entered its imperialist phase at the turn of the century. The struggle had begun for the redistribution of raw materials and spheres of influence, and it was this struggle that drove mankind into war. The international workers' movements, including those of women, tried to counteract

these developments. However, before the first international congress of socialist women took place in August 1907, a great revolutionary event burst upon the world, demanding the active solidarity of all socialist women: the first Russian insurrection of 1904 and 1905.

In the bloody struggle of the Russian working class against feudalism and the reactionary tsarist system, many Russian women gave their freedom and even their lives.

The revolutionary storms which weakened the repressive tsarist regime at the same time made thousands of women, until then silent and repressed, into passionate fighters. This period prepared the ground for what was to happen a decade later. The Russian writer Maxim Gorky has described this process in his book, *Mother*.

All over the world there were many who sympathized with the Russian rebels. Clara Zetkin, through her late husband, particularly closely allied to the Russian revolutionaries, was one of the initiators of this movement. Her newspaper was completely at the service of solidarity with the Russian Revolution. It explained the revolution to the people, asking them to learn from this spectacular rising, and to study the methods of struggle. Among these new methods were above all public demonstrations, not only parading the growing strength of working men and women but at the same time invigorating them through the realization of their own strength.

Economic strikes turned into political ones. The Russian working class no longer fought just for a few extra kopecks; their aim was now more democracy, more freedom and more rights. A wave of massive strikes which

shook several European countries in 1905 and 1906 had been set in motion by the revolutionary events in Russia. When these were bloodily suppressed by the tsarist regime, women were among the many victims. Side by side with their men, they marched the dreaded trail to banishment into the endless wastes of Siberia.

The first international congress of socialist women, in August 1907, was attended by fifty-six delegates from fourteen countries: Germany, Russia, Italy, France, Holland, Belgium, Sweden, Norway, Hungary, Switzerland, the United States, Britain, Bohemia, and Finland. They chose Clara Zetkin as their secretary, and *Die Gleichheit* became an international paper. Impressive as the conference was, it also revealed the existence of opportunism in the international workers' movement, which was about to undermine its unity. Yet, wom-

en's fighting strength was increased against exploitation, against a split in the workers' movement, and the ever growing danger of war apparent in the emergence of two power blocks and the general militarization of life.

A few years later, in 1910, another international conference of women in Copenhagen decided to hold an International Women's Day each year, in March. This day was to serve as a demonstration for women's suffrage. But beyond that it became a day of fighting spirit for women's equality, peace and socialism. None of the women assembled in Copenhagen could have realized that their resolution would eventually bring together millions of women in all parts of the world.

As early as March 1911, a million men and women in Denmark, Germany, Austria and Switzerland attended mass meetings on Inter-

national Women's Day. In all industrialized countries thousands of women now joined the workers' movement. In Germany the number of female party members rose in the years from 1908 to 1914 from about 62,000 to 167,000.

Yet, in spite of all the efforts of the revolutionary social democrats, in spite of consistent action of the Left against treason inside the workers' movement, in spite of the untiring work of Karl Liebknecht, Rosa Luxemburg, and Clara Zetkin for internationalism and solidarity of workers in all countries, World War I broke out in 1914, and the leadership of the German social democrats threw in their lot with the imperialist defenders of the Fatherland. This treason, prepared by opportunist forces in the international movement, was a heavy blow to socialist women, the heaviest of all to that day.

Uprising of the people against the unbearable yoke of capitalists and landlords. 140,000 St Petersburg workers marched, still believing in their 'little father', the Tsar. They marched with church banners and icons to the Winter Palace. Among the thousands, lying bleeding, mowed down by the Tsar's guns, were women, many women, and children...

Then everywhere in Russia great strikes flared up, and women, too, were leading them, Russian women, till now despised, humbled, jeered at with the words of "the hen being no bird..."

Down with War

Railway carriages scribbled with chauvinist slogans took the youth of Germany off to the battlefields. And this in a country which had boasted a strong workers' movement, filled with the spirit of genuine internationalism. Many socialist women, not seized by war frenzy, watched this spectacle in despair. There was only one country, Russia, with a party of fighting Marxists free from opportunism. From the very first the Russian working class was alerted to the struggle against imperialist war. In Germany a revolutionary nucleus of thinking men and women was drawn further to the Left. This circle's most outstanding personalities were Karl Liebknecht, Rosa Luxemburg, Clara Zetkin and the writer Franz Mehring. In social-democratic papers abroad this group disassociated itself from the lie that German social democrats stood united behind the country's defense. Inside Germany all opposition was suppressed and it was therefore extremely difficult to explain fully the nature of the war, and to organize the tasks of socialists in the struggle against mass murder. All the same, right from the beginning, women workers, many young girls among them, joined the ranks of anti-war fighters. In November 1914 Clara Zetkin wrote to British women socialists who had sent a message of solidarity to Germany: "We, the socialist women of all countries, recognize imperialism as the enemy which has now set one people against another ... This imperialism can never make a pact with socialism. We are therefore determined to employ the full strength of our will and the fervor of our hearts to make socialism overcome imperialism ..."

In spite of all difficulties, Clara Zetkin managed to organize a congress of socialist women in Berne late in March 1915. There were twenty-five delegates, from Britain, France, Germany, Russia, Italy, Poland, the Netherlands, and Switzerland. They decided on a manifesto to the women of all nations, unmasking the imperialist character of the war, and calling on the women of the warring countries to unite. The representative from Russia, Nadezhda Krupskaya, presented a resolution to the congress, outlined by Lenin. It pointed towards the transformation of the imperialist war into a revolutionary civil war. The majority of the women present were not ready yet to join in such a definitive declaration, and it became very obvious at the time that international socialism had developed its chief revolutionary impulse in Russia.

A few days before the conference, on March 18th, 1915, hundreds of women had demonstrated in front of the *Reichstag* building in Germany, many of them in mourning and some with their children. They had the courage to address the representatives of the bourgeois parties, demanding: "Give us back our husbands, fathers and brothers. We want peace." This demonstration was repeated on May 28th, when two thousand women took part and the police harshly attacked women and children with rubber truncheons. In the same year Rosa Luxemburg said in a brochure written in prison, published under the pen name Junius (21): "The scene has changed completely. The march to Paris within six weeks has turned into a drama of world dimension, mass slaughter has become a tedious daily business ... The intoxication is over! And the patriotic noise in the streets ..."

Clara Zetkin, too, was imprisoned in July 1915, "attempted treason" was the charge. Because of her poor health she was released in October and, disregarding her physical condition, she immediately took up the struggle again. In 1916 and 1917 demonstrations against the war increased, and the February revolution in Russia gave a mighty impetus to anti-war actions. It also accelerated the renewed move towards the Left of the international workers' movement, and gave hope to millions of people. Inside the social-democratic parties sharp ideological arguments took place, leading in time to a complete break between revolutionary socialists and social democrats. In connection with these arguments, when Clara Zetkin uncompromisingly defended her revolutionary position, the leadership of the social democrats relieved her of the editorship of *Die Gleichheit*, following underhand attacks against the paper. After twenty-five years of a brave stand for the cause of women and the whole socialist movement, the paper now became an opportunist publication of the right wing of the party. This was a hard blow against the socialist women's movement and the person of its most distinguished leader. Clara Zetkin took it undismayed. She, like Rosa Luxemburg, was at that time completely taken up with the events in Russia. "It is true," she wrote, "that the imperialist World War has strutted through history for fully four years, destroying, and leaving its bloody trail, accompanied by the shameful bankruptcy of the Second International. Yet, in history something

ROSA LUXEMBURG

She was an eagle of the revolution.
Loved by millions
just as her enemies hated "Red Rosa".
She had the brave heart of the fighter,
calling a time wonderful which threw up
"masses of problems, mighty problems",
bringing forth "gigantic things".

But she might be late arriving to discuss
these gigantic things, because a child,
weeping, had kept her.

And from prison which was to check
the eagle's flight, she wrote enchantingly
about animals and colored stones,
and the dandelion, with
"so much sun in its color..."

Rosa Luxemburg was killed.
"Killed by the orders
of German oppressors,"
Bertolt Brecht wrote, and added:
"Oppressed, bury your discord..."

mightier has taken place: the proletarian revolution has come into being in the former tsarist empire ..." (22)

The revolution also proved a watershed in the history of the socialist women workers' movement. Their best traditions were taken over by the communist parties forming all over the world. "In these communist parties," Clara Zetkin wrote, "working-class women must not be left out. They carry the invigorating tradition of years of valiant struggle." And indeed, women played an active part in the class struggle of the next decade. They helped to obtain their vote, and walked next to the men behind the coffins of their murdered leaders, Karl Liebknecht and Rosa Luxemburg. Their mourning turned into energy and the will to fight. When the Republic of Soviets was founded in Hungary in March 1919, a great number of women and young girls joined the new Communist Party, lead by Béla Kún. In the 133 days of worker's power in Hungary, women were present on all fronts, defending the republic at the side of their men. In the factories they proved that a socialist republic can function, and at a worker's university they organized communist training. Women and girls were among the martyrs when the republic succumbed to Hungarian and international reactionary forces, and a terrific bloodbath ended the people's rising.

All over Europe socialist women proved their solidarity with the Soviets, now threatened from many directions. They demonstrated in tens of thousands under the slogan "Hands off Soviet Russia!" In September 1923 the Bulgarian people rose in a revolutionary attempt at liberation. Many courageous women joined the fight, carrying the wounded from a rain of bullets, taking messages on horseback from division to division, or throwing themselves into the armed struggle side by side with the men. As in Hungary, they shared in the revolution's collapse, suffered torture, exile and death with their male comrades. The names of brave women of that September have entered the history of the Bulgarian people: Zola Dragoitsheva, Rada Todorova, and Georgina Karastojanova.

In many countries women were the tireless helpers of International Red Aid. Like their grandmothers before them under the anti-socialist law, they helped to supply the families of prisoners with food, fuel, clothes and money. Everywhere socialist women were among the most active organizers of strikes, and actual strikers themselves during the hard years of the world-wide economic crisis. Together with progressive doctors they fought for legalization of abortion which was then still heavily punishable, a fact which often meant great worry and danger to the families of workers.

In the German workers' movement women were ready to fight the rising fascism, and from their ranks came some of the heroines who later risked their lives in the resistance against the Hitler regime.

QUESTIONS
TO THE WIFE OF A WORKER

Are you a good comrade,
walking by his side,
accompanying his every step,
fighting against oppression?

Do you hold him back
when red flags call?
He fights for happiness
for you and him.
Be at his side! Be at his side!
Up to new heights.

Kurt Tucholsky

Max Lingner. Down with war. 1934

Making
Dreams
Come True

Revolution

"I have seen nothing but my husband, known nothing but beatings, work and fear ..."

At the age of forty Pelagueya Vlasova, the heroine of Gorky's novel, *Mother*, is, like all her working-class contemporaries, an old woman, "a little mother". She tries to understand the barbaric world in which she is forced to live. She tries to understand why woman is a despised being, why neither father, husband nor sons show her kindness or love. She decides that they despise woman because they themselves are despised. They are so low in their own misery that there is only one being more lowly than themselves—woman.

"He beats me ... as if he wasn't just beating his wife, but everybody he was furious about ..."

Great backwardness and deep ignorance marked the life of the Russian woman of the people. The yoke of tsarist rule weighed on her shoulders most heavily. She was the most oppressed and most exploited creature in pre-revolutionary Russia, used from childhood to bend her back first before her father, then before the lord of the manor, her husband, and, of course, the priest. Her social position was well expressed in a proverb: "The hen is no bird, and woman not a human being," words known to every male in the tsarist empire. Eighty per cent of all wage-earning women were unskilled day laborers or employed in domestic service. Thirteen per cent worked for starvation wages in industry or on building sites, and only four per cent worked in education.

It can be seen quite clearly now that the revolution meant a great deal more to Russian women than merely the satisfaction of the elemental wish for peace, bread and land. It meant the beginning of liberation from deepest degradation.

But to what extent could Russian women at that time—in the fateful year of 1917—take the step from passive suffering to awareness of the significance of the revolution?

There were in fact millions who could not understand the cause of their situation: the relation of individual destiny to the system in power. Yet, wherever there was fighting, women were in the struggle. Many took a very simple view of the revolution. To them, it finished the cursed war; husbands and sons would return home, and the revolution would give land to the people and food to the children. We have guns, they thought, and whatever happens, we must not go back to what has been.

One of these women, Marcjanna Fornalska, wrote the story of her life for her granddaughter when she was eighty, still hardly knowing the alphabet and therefore groping for every letter on the typewriter. It made a touching book, now widely read by young and old. Her children, says the author, had to help her understand what was going on in the October Revolution. They told her that Soviet power would mean a government for the poorest among the poor, a government for the people. "I did not understand much," continues Marcjanna, "but what my children said, I thought, must be true. They were educated at school, and the facts were sacred to me ... The path they trod, I longed to tread also ..."

And indeed, she overcame her deep-seated fear of her mistress, and went out into the streets with the masses. "Instinctively we felt that something great and joyful was happening. Now, as I am writing it down, I am eighty years of age, and I have seen much sorrow but also much joy. Yet, never did I have that strange feeling again ... just as if a new world opened before me. And that is exactly what it was ... I was born again."

Very young girls joined the determined revolutionaries. Anna Kolpakova and Ekaterina Karmanova, two grey-haired Moscow women, their spirits still young, gave me a personal account of those stormy days. They were friends, full of dreams, enthusiastic about Bebel's book, *Woman and Socialism*. The revolution was their first test under fire. Like many of their young friends, they were used as scouts. Smiling, they recollected consulting a book on the revolution of 1905 to find out how such a rebellion was made anyway.

There was a third friend of theirs, Lisya Lisinovska, who was not contented with discovering cells of "white Russians" or establishing medical depots. She demanded a gun. She got it, and was shot herself, in a cowardly manner from a window, on the day after. Now a street bears her name: Lisinovskaya.

Side by side with the many unknown women of the people there fought highly educated ones, well-versed in revolutionary tactics. Nadezhda Krupskaya, Lenin's brave companion, was among them. Under the hard conditions of exile she had undertaken important tasks for the preparation of the revolution. Later, after victory, the whole strength of this unusual woman belonged to the creation and

NADEZHDA KRUPSKAYA

He just called her Nadya.
Steady and sensitive
in learning
and in teaching
she conquered
the web of illiteracy.
Brains became clearer
and life in the cottages brighter.
Nadezhda Krupskaya,
though without pretension,
she was never content
with her times,
and left us with
the gains
of a rich
shared life.

Lisa Jobst

development of a new progressive socialist system of education.

Another unforgettable woman of the revolution was Alexandra Kollontai, a Russian comrade of Clara Zetkin and Rosa Luxemburg. While still young, she had chosen the path of a revolutionary although she belonged to the privileged family of a tsarist general. In 1917 she became a member of the Executive Committee of the Bolsheviks and sat on the Council of the People's Commissars after the revolution, with special responsibility for the building up of the new social services. Later her abilities and experience fitted her to become the Soviet Union's first woman ambassador, representing her country in Norway, Mexico and Sweden.

The courageous actions of women and their readiness for sacrifice greatly contributed to the success of the October Revolution. Long before, Lenin had written: "The experience of all movements for national liberation has shown that the success of a revolution depends on the extent to which women take part in it." (23)

The October Revolution was the great rebellion of the oppressed carried through to the end. It destroyed exploitation at the roots, putting in its place an order which liberated one hundred million tormented people. Half of them, former subjects of the Tsar, were women, and the Soviet government immediately after victory repealed all laws prejudicial to women or discriminating against them. Men and women were to have equal rights.

This was in accord with the theories of Marx and Engels and with the scientific foresight of August Bebel and Clara Zetkin.

The absolute relation between socialist revolution and the liberation of women had so far existed in theory only, a demand, not a reality. It is true that even as a theory it activated thousands of people, and in that way became a force to be reckoned with. But now the proof of the correctness of the theory was to be found. The liberation of women was no longer an ideal to be looked for but an urgent task, the solution of which meant a revolution within a revolution.

Immediately after the October Revolution, laws were issued completely changing the social position of woman.

One of the most important of these laws was the decree introducing equal pay for equal work. It ended discrimination against female labor which in Russia, too, had been a great source of employers' profits. Until the revolution the average daily wage of a male laborer had been one rouble and forty-one kopecks, while a woman earned about half of this starvation pay, seventy-two kopecks, for the same work.

By another decree men and women obtained one free day a week, and an eight-hour-day ended the torment of the long drawn out working hours particularly taxing to women, who nearly always had to take care of the family in addition to their employment. A true present to working men and women was a decree on holidays granting them an annual vacation with full pay.

It was characteristic of the serious endeavor of the revolutionary government that it strove to improve woman's position in every area, and at the same time took measures for the protection of the working woman. Women

MARCJANNA FORNALSKA

At the age of eighty, she,
a simple Polish woman, and
still barely literate,
wrote down her memories
for her granddaughter,
laboriously seeking each letter
on the typewriter, with one finger.
Her writings made a book,
"Memories of a Mother",
read since by thousands with emotion.
And of the October Revolution
she said: "I was born again."

were no longer allowed to work in industries likely to damage their health. Limits were established for the carrying and heaving of weights by women. Lenin himself, soon after the revolution, signed the historic *Decree for the Protection of Mother and Child*. For the first time in history a country developed an inclusive system for the care of pregnant women and mothers, planned completely for their protection. Many orders substantiated this important decree.

At the end of 1917, it was decreed that women for a stated time before and after delivery were to be released from work, and were to receive pay, free medical attention for mother and child, and full guarantee of return to their job. Where breast-feeding of the child was possible near the place of work, the working mother was given a paid break of half an hour, every three hours.

About the same time, on December 31st, 1917, the Soviet government issued decrees on marriage, children and divorce which were an essential basis for diminishing the inequality of women in the family. They recognized civil marriage, settled the equality of legitimate and illegitimate children, and gave women the right to establish paternity and sue the father of a child.

When discussing the Soviet measures concerning the liberation of women, Lenin could rightly say in 1920: "In two years of Soviet power the most backward country in Europe did more for woman's liberation and making her an equal of the stronger sex than all the progressive and enlightened democratic republics of the whole world put together have ever done." (24)

ALEXANDRA KOLLONTAI

Abroad she was often called
"the eighth wonder of the world".
Because of her beauty?
Or because she,
the daughter of a wealthy
Tsar's general,
chose the hard way of
a revolutionary?
Or because
in the year of the Revolution
she became the first woman commissar,
and later
the first woman ambassador
of the Soviet Union?
She was no "wonder of the world".
She was
a specially brave
and specially clever,
specially lovable citizen
of her liberated country.

Tygrena and Chaditsha

Anyone who wants to understand the full significance of the "Russian miracle" must take into account the vastness of the country and its diversity, the many different languages and the differences in cultural development of the Soviet Union's many peoples.

It is – as can be seen even now – not easy fully to achieve woman's equality in spite of favorable conditions under a socialist regime. And at the time of the revolution the difficulties of solving the problem were enormous, considering the large areas of Russia still in an incredibly backward state. The peoples of the Soviet Union were in greatly varying stages of social evolution, the more progressive ones in industrial areas, the others mainly inhabitants of marginal regions, still clinging to a feudal or even more primitive social order.

To take one example, the road to equality was very complicated for the peoples of northeast Siberia. For a long time after the revolution, regions several times the size of Western Europe held stubbornly to many forms of labor and family tradition which dated back to primitive society. Among the Chukchee in the far northwest, and the Koryaki, the Kamchadales and related tribes living farther to the west, primitive industry was limited to reindeer breeding, fishing and hunt-

*Every day
the men gave thanks to Allah
for not having been born a woman.
And they knew why.
Woman had to serve
five masters
in the Russian Orient:
God, the Khan, the Bey,
the Mullah,
and her husband.
She looked on the world
through a grating of horsehair
the window of the harem
which separated her
from life outside.*

"Revolution of manners" meant
the victory of freedom.
But victory came
at the end of a fierce struggle.
Ten years after the October Revolution
two hundred and fifty women
were killed in Uzbekistan.

Their crime:
they had uncovered their faces,
shown them to the new world,
unveiled.

ing. Many tribes living in the northeast were robbed of the results of their labor by American traders who came in whole "caravans" across the Bering Straits, only eighty-six kilometers wide. They unscrupulously exploited the ignorance and trust of the natives of the Chukchee peninsula, obtaining precious furs in the cheapest way and at the same time drawing the inhabitants into a vicious net of debts.

The Russian anthropologist Suev has described the situation of women among the people of the tundra: "It is impossible to imagine in what low esteem the female sex is held. I venture to say that with them women do not live like human beings, but like necessary domestic animals one cannot do without."

Other scholars reported differences in the position of women in different tribes. With the Nentsy, for example, women possessed a certain amount of independence which was founded not least on the possession of their own reindeers. In many groups mothers enjoyed care and respect. But there might exist in the same group primitive customs which degraded women as "unclean". Thus every dwelling place of the Nentsy had a special room, a sacred place, which no woman was allowed to enter because she would pollute it and make it unclean. Women were not allowed to cross

*For the first time
in a doctor's waiting room.
Perhaps fear and superstition
have not been overcome altogether.
Yet everybody remembers
a word by Lenin
which has become a program:*
EVERYTHING FOR THE
CHILD.
*And the word is stronger than fear.
It is a key to the hearts of mothers.*

the road in front of a dog-drawn sledge, nor hang their clothes next to men's. If a woman stepped over a rein, harness, gun or any other item belonging to a man, the article became useless. Woman had to give birth alone, in a remote place. Whoever helped her, the "unclean" one, offended against the mighty unwritten law.

It is useless to moralize about customs and habits of this kind, as it is easy to come to hasty and non-scientific conclusions. These customs do not arise from the evil behavior of man towards woman, nor do they result from individual cruelty; rather they belong to an early state of economic and cultural development. Nevertheless, primitive ways of thought and action often outlast their origins, and persist for a long time under new and more favorable circumstances. In the end, of course, with the constant confrontation of old and new they disappear.

Soviet novels show even more clearly than the reports of scholars the life of women in

Siberia's northeast. An example is a scene from Siomushkin's *Fire in the Polar Night*: In the Chukchee peninsula of northeast Siberia a Soviet Committee has recently settled and its representatives call the inhabitants of the country to a court hearing. They arrive from all directions with their dog sledges, for a case agitating all their minds is to be decided on.

A young woman, Tygrena, has run away from her unloved husband, and has asked the revolutionary committee for protection. And now she has to explain, before all the people assembled, why she does not want to return to her husband, Alitet. Alitet, who is also present, tries to keep Tygrena from speaking. "Chief," he says to the chairman of the committee, "she is a woman ... Why do you ask her? Does the master ask the dog where it wants to go? Has she forgotten that I have paid the bride money for her? I have given her father four dogs ..." But Tygrena is allowed to speak, and overcoming her shyness about

*Medicine
in the Altai mountains,
only a generation ago,
meant the mumblings of a shaman,
the drumming of the tambourine,
and animal sacrifice...
To this young woman doctor
all that seems
a thousand years ago.*

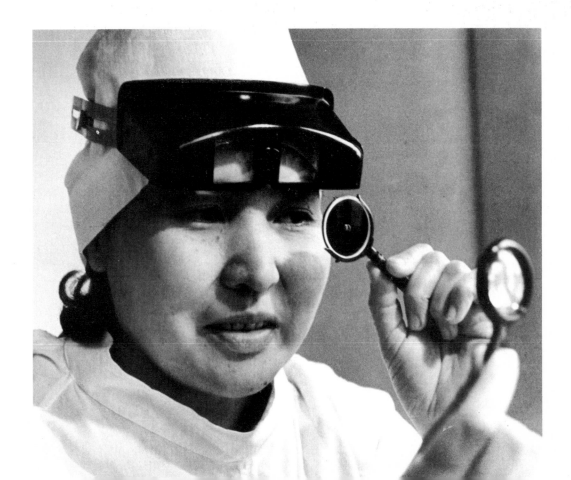

speaking freely in front of men, she tells how Alitet, the trader, a tool of the American dealers driven out by the revolution, had used the fact of her father being in debt to take her by force. She tells how at times he put her at the disposal of his guests and how she fled, and again and again was brought back. Living together with her husband's two other wives had become unbearable. The other two kept together like the fingers of a hand, "but I was sent hunting all the time," relates the heroine. "Shivering I sat in the pack-ice, but I did not want to go home ..."

The verdict of the court was something unheard of, something that had never happened before: the court protected the woman. The marriage was dissolved, and part of Alitet's property was confiscated and given to Tygrena.

This scene from the novel allows the reader to guess what the revolution meant to the lives of women in similar circumstances. Siomushkin has only portrayed with the means at the writer's disposal what he found in real life. There were many Tygrenas, and during a period of less than a lifespan they moved from primitive conditions to those of a modern socialist state. They overcame the many difficulties of understanding this new life, adjusting themselves to meet its demands, and in time helping to shape it. The charming, intelligent and self-confident young women from the Siberian north and northeast are today skilled workers. They are animal breeders, engineers, geologists, teachers or doctors in their homelands, or they study at the universities of Yakutsk, Irkutsk, Arkhangelsk, Leningrad or Moscow. As the daughters and granddaughters

of the generation of Tygrena they have come a long way.

Looking at the liberation of women in the Soviet Union, it is also necessary to take account of the areas referred to as the "Russian Orient". Many of the peoples there formerly lived under feudalism. Feudal rulers, their officials and governors, supported by Mohammedan priests, kept the people in bondage. This power also shaped the women's life. They had, said a proverb, five masters to rule over them: God, the Khan, the Bey, the Mullah, and the husband. Ancestors' customs were law to their descendants. This meant child marriage, unlimited power for the husband, and polygamy for the wealthy. Because woman, like a domestic animal, was the property of the husband, he could kill her at the slightest suspicion of unfaithfulness, without being punished for the murder. The woman, however, was threatened with prison if she passed from her husband's threshold unveiled.

The Soviet government had to press the liberation of women among the peoples of Turkestan both carefully and determinedly. (25) Discrimination against women was deeply rooted in Mohammedan faith and the Bolsheviks could not act rashly in a region where for centuries millions had blindly followed the teachings of Islam.

Yet, as early as 1918 the Soviet government issued a decree giving the women of the country the right to discard their traditional garments and veil. (26) At the same time they were encouraged to work and to train. In 1922 further laws made illegal the buying and selling of girls, and with it the paying of bride money. The legal age for marriage of girls—

who were often sold to a man at nine years of age—was raised to sixteen.

To live according to these new and progressive laws required much courage from older and younger women. They were, for instance, ruthlessly persecuted and punished like criminals when they dared to attend one of the newly opened schools. In the 1920's the Soviet government had not yet obtained a firm foothold in these regions, and therefore could not enforce the new laws and protect women from injustice. For years the government was involved in fierce struggles with hostile gangs of the once powerful Khans and Beys. But there were also many obstacles and prejudices to be overcome which originated in the women's own minds. Clara Zetkin, who in 1924 and 1928 did educational work among women in Mohammedan clubs, wrote: "Between their desire to do things and their actual activities there is the invisible latticed window of the harem."

The revolution of customs and manners claimed bloody victims. As late as 1927 two hundred and fifty women were murdered in Uzbekistan because they had discarded the veil. Still, and in spite of all terror, *Chudsum*, the movement of women against the wearing of the traditional garment, could not be defeated.

A woman brought up in Kazakhstan, a region of Central Asia large enough to take in West and Central Europe, may speak for herself: "My name is Chaditsha Jesenturova Mursalieva. I was born in 1914 in Kyzyl-Orda, at the northern edge of the Kyzyl Kum desert ... In the Kazakh steppes people lived as they had done in pre-historic times. They came into the world in a tent, and only the fittest would survive diseases, epidemics, dirt and the ignorance of their own mothers. Of a thousand children in Kazakhstan five hundred died before they were three years old. If one did survive, and if one was a girl, one learned to bake bread and to spin wool. When the time had come, one was married to a man chosen by the father, who received the bride money. Then one bore children of one's own, brought them up, and became old before one had ever been young. If the husband died, one became the property of his nearest relation, like a domestic animal ... I, too, was to be married when I was fourteen years old. But I did not want to live as my grandmother and my mother had been forced to live. Ideas, possibilities and circumstances, brought about with Soviet rule, helped me to free myself from the past. I belonged to the Young Pioneers, and I wanted to learn. I ran away from home, and travelled by train more than a thousand kilometers to the north."

This girl, Chaditsha, went to school, then to the university, first becoming a doctor, then a lecturer and director of the Second Women's Hospital of the Medical University at Alma Ata, the capital of Kazakhstan.

Literacy became the deciding factor in overcoming backwardness in all matters, including the relationship of the sexes. This was not true only for the marginal regions but applied to all the vast territories of the Soviet Union. Everywhere one of the main revolutionary tasks was the struggle for education, knowledge and culture.

The tsarist regime had spent on education a mere eighty kopecks per capita and year, and 76 of every hundred people could neither read nor write. Among the female population between nine and forty-nine years of age the percentage of illiteracy was even greater, 87%.

But the electrification of the vast country, the building up of modern industry and the change from the horse to the tractor could not be effected by illiterate people. Education was as necessary for these wider issues as it was for personal human relationships.

The Cook and the Multiplication Tables

In December 1917 the Council of the People's Commissars published a decree for the abolition of illiteracy. This made it the duty of all citizens between eight and fifty years of age, men and women, to learn to read and write. They could do so according to choice in their own or in the Russian language. All those concerned were to have their working day shortened by two hours but receive full pay. A vast network for administering the system was established. Those who could read and write were obliged to teach others. Of interest is the fact that hundreds and thousands of children became the teachers of their parents and grandparents. Seven million people, among them four million women, learned to read and write in the years between 1917 and 1920. After seizing power the revolutionaries' zeal included their ambition for knowledge and education. Mayakovsky encouraged them by saying: "Workers and peasants, your enemies are all armed with knowledge. You have defeated their institutions, but in order to reap the fruits of victory you must yourselves attain knowledge. Only then will the future be yours."

And the people began their way out of the darkness of ignorance. There are many contemporary documents illustrating how these first groping steps were taken. One is the photograph of a young woman standing by a blackboard displaying a simple lesson in

Before the Siberian Altai region
became the Autonomous Mountain
Republic of Altai,
its inhabitants did not possess
a written language.
They did not have a word for "book"
or "school" or "doctor" . . .

Today for every thousand
inhabitants of Altai
there are more students
than for every thousand citizens
of the United States of America.

arithmetic which a class of adults is struggling to solve.

In many villages and settlements the school was the first properly built house. Village reading rooms became attractive meeting places for men and women after work was done, more so even for women than for men. These rooms became centers of the awakening intellectual and political life, with everyone eager to participate.

Lenin's words that the cook needed to learn how to rule were understood more easily by simple women than by the many foreign journalists and writers who misinterpreted them. The women took those words as a challenge to each one of them, even the one time "lowest", to learn to understand the world, and then be able to help in shaping it. The Soviet constitution of 1918 guaranteed women the same civic rights as men. For the first time in Russia's history they could vote and be elected to the local and highest offices of the state. But how were they to implement this political equality, how take an active part in the life of society, when they lacked all knowledge and immediate experience?

Generally, together with knowledge grew perception. Together with letters and numbers, millions learned to think out problems posed by the new situation affecting their lives. It was then that they became aware of the power of their own minds.

Fedor Gladkov in his well-known book of the 1920's, *Cement*, shows clearly the effects of growing literacy, particularly on women.

He describes how in the first lesson arranged to combat illiteracy in a cement factory, completely disorganized by war, the whole audience consisted of women. Dasha, Gladkov's lovable heroine, member of the women's committee, impressed her future pupils by saying that women compared to men were the more active fighters in the struggle for education. What mattered was not just to learn to read and write, but to acquire that true self-education which would guide them in coping with the key problems of an emergent state. Knowledge was power, and without it no country could be ruled. "And the women," continued Gladkov, "must become aware of their social import, and begin to feel that their stature would grow culturally and politically, a long way from the kitchen sink ..."

The woman manager of a modern store on Moscow's Lenin Prospekt, Nina Korshilova, remembers: "My mother was a very simple uneducated working woman. In the twenties, when hunger for knowledge seized the masses, she began to read and write enthusiastically, even with passion. Later she went to the university and became an art historian and deputy director of the Tretyakov Gallery."

Apart from this single case, by 1926 literacy in the Soviet Union had risen from 24% to 51.5%, and in 1934 there were only ten in one hundred people—and they were mostly old—who could not read or write. Many considered the victory over illiteracy, next to that over foreign intervention, the greatest achievement of the early years of Soviet government.

Even now Western visitors to the Soviet Union are impressed with the great love for reading among old and young, and their veneration of books. However, in view of the development of education in Russia, this is a perfectly understandable phenomenon.

A completely new system of education gave every child in the country an equal chance to be educated, and enabled him in time to take part in the progress of the arts and sciences. This was an enormous task, considering that some of the Soviet peoples did not even possess a written language, and that in "Oriental Russia" conditions were medieval. In vast parts of the Soviet Union there were many millions who had never seen an electric bulb, an engine or even a house built of stone.

And all these gigantic tasks had to be undertaken in years of starvation and under extreme difficulties in a country left devastated by the war.

The Front is Everywhere

In 1918 when the government issued a call to arms under the slogan: "Our socialist Fatherland is in danger", the enemy was attacking on all fronts. There were also enemies inside the country in league with the foreign enemy.

Many women followed the call, and volunteered for the Red Army.

Marcjanna Fornalska describes in her writings how her daughters enlisted: "My heart throbbed when I looked at my young daughter. She was only sixteen, slim and delicate like a child ... Shortly after, my elder daughter, too, joined the Tsaritsyn Communist Battalion, leaving her small son in my care."

Girls and boys of the communist youth organizations, still filled with the spirit of the revolutionary events, never hesitated to take up arms. They did much to encourage others. "The district committee is closed. Everyone is at the front", was the legend on the door of many offices in those days. Outside intervention and civil war became an everyday problem for the government, and a trial of strength for all the people.

In 1919 when the White Russians, under the leadership of General Yudenich, attacked Petrograd, numbers of women fought in the medical branch, in the signal and pioneer corps. They dug trenches, renewed defense installations, and proved themselves in the armed defense of their city. Others cared for the families of soldiers and orphaned children, or worked in communal kitchens. We do not know how many women sat in the saddle daily, riding from one section of the front to the next, rifle over one shoulder, medical bag slung over the other, always facing death, always ready to risk their lives, risk anything rather than go back to the past.

A large part of the former tsarist empire fell temporarily into the hands of the counter-revolutionaries. In the regions occupied by the enemy, there rose a strong partisan movement in which many women fought, taking upon themselves great risks and sacrifices. Nearly all male communists were at the front, and therefore in many places women did the resistance work, like Dasha in *Cement* providing their knowledge, a talent for organizing and great bravery.

The most cruel scourge of those years was hunger. Kolchak's troops had cut the country off from its granary on the Volga, and there was war in the other grain-growing areas. Every day in towns and villages women and children died of starvation. A million or more were killed by epidemics. The lament of Motya in Gladkov's novel is typical: "I have had children, I was a happy mother. Where are they now—our children have perished—can one live on like that? I cry myself to death; I can't go on. I'll go into the street, and fetch home some orphans."

Abandoned, homeless children haunted the countryside, always hungry, always searching for a crumb of bread.

The economy was shattered. The few workers who had remained in the factories could hardly keep on their feet because of hunger. About that time, in April 1919, a group of Moscow workers made a decision which Lenin called "the beginning of a change". On Saturday, April 12th, they remained in the factory at the close of work, and in ten hours of unpaid work they repaired three locomotives for the front. That was the birth of the communist *Subbotniks*—work on Saturday—a mass movement including great numbers of women. They helped with the providing of fuel, the cleaning of the streets, schools and barracks, and the building of day nurseries for children. From May 1920 to March 1921 in Moscow alone 250,000 women took part in the *Subbotniks*. This movement, in a situation of emergency and economic disorder, gave courage and strength to people, and became one of the causes of final victory.

The revolution had come to stay. The superhuman effort and sacrifice of a whole people beat the enemy without and within.

In January 1920 Lenin wrote to a congress of women in Petrograd: "We will now successfully finish the civil war ... From now on the Soviet government has to concentrate its strength on a task closer and more familiar to us: the unbloody war, the victory over hunger, cold and destruction. In this unbloody war women in town and country are called upon to play a special part." (27)

Red Kerchiefs

The country was shattered by foreign invasion and civil war. In 1920 the Soviet Republic's agriculture supplied less than half of its pre-war production, and in spite of worker's intense efforts heavy industrial output was seven times less than before the war. Lenin said of the Russia of this period that its condition could be compared to that of a man half beaten to death. "The country has been beaten for seven years, and may the Lord grant it can move if only with crutches. That is exactly the situation we find ourselves in."

All the same the people's courage and optimism were unbeatable. They were, it was said, as if made of iron. Perhaps there is no better example of this confident hope than the historic manifestation which Aleksey Nikolayevich Tolstoy has strikingly described in his novel, *The Road to Calvary*.

It happened in 1920 when men and women assembled at the Bolshoi Theatre in Moscow, shivering with cold and exhaustion, but listening with fascinated attention to the theme of the day: the building up of the country, and particularly its electrification. A huge map of European Russia hung at the back of the stage, covered with colored circles and dots. In front of it stood the speaker, an engineer. "Here," he said, "where in the thousands of years old silence of Russia millions of tons of peat are hidden, here where there is a waterfall or a mighty river, we shall build power stations—lighthouses, as it were, of common enterprise ..." and he lifted his stick to point to future centers of energy. And like stars these points lit up in the darkness of the large stage. To be able to light up this map for a few seconds, it had been necessary to concentrate all the energy of the Moscow power station. For the length of the lecture Moscow was plunged into darkness, with only one light bulb even burning in the Kremlin. People in the auditorium, carrying a handful of oats in their pockets, the day's ration instead of bread, listened, holding their breath, listened to what perspectives the revolution held out for them. A beginning had been made.

The peoples of Russia, so religious at one time, no longer expected their salvation from a higher being or the wisdom of a government, good as it might be. They knew that a better life could only come through the labor of them all. In a speech in front of women workers Lenin had made clear that "this work the Soviet government has begun can only go forward when all over Russia not hundreds but millions and millions of women take a part in it."

The participation of women in the building up of the country, their inclusion in productive work, was at the same time the most important condition for woman's emancipation. Only in productive work beyond her family circle could she recognize her abilities, and gain material independence from the despotism of her breadwinner husband. Even in these early days there were some remarkable initiatives by Russian women. The women of the Yartsev textile factory (in the Smolensk district), for example, decided to get hundreds of machines back into working condition. For months on end, after eight hours of hard work, the women stayed behind voluntarily to clean, repair

Following double page:

There is war. Civil war.
Millions are starving.
Thousands die.
Yet, the great LEARNING
has begun;
fifty million people
have ceased to be illiterate.
205 plus 315? Tomorrow
it will no longer be a problem.
Pale children guide
grandmother's hand.
Young girls
go to remote villages,
to carry knowledge
into the cottages.
And proudly
they call their work:
"Fighting on the third front."
And their enemy:
Ignorance.

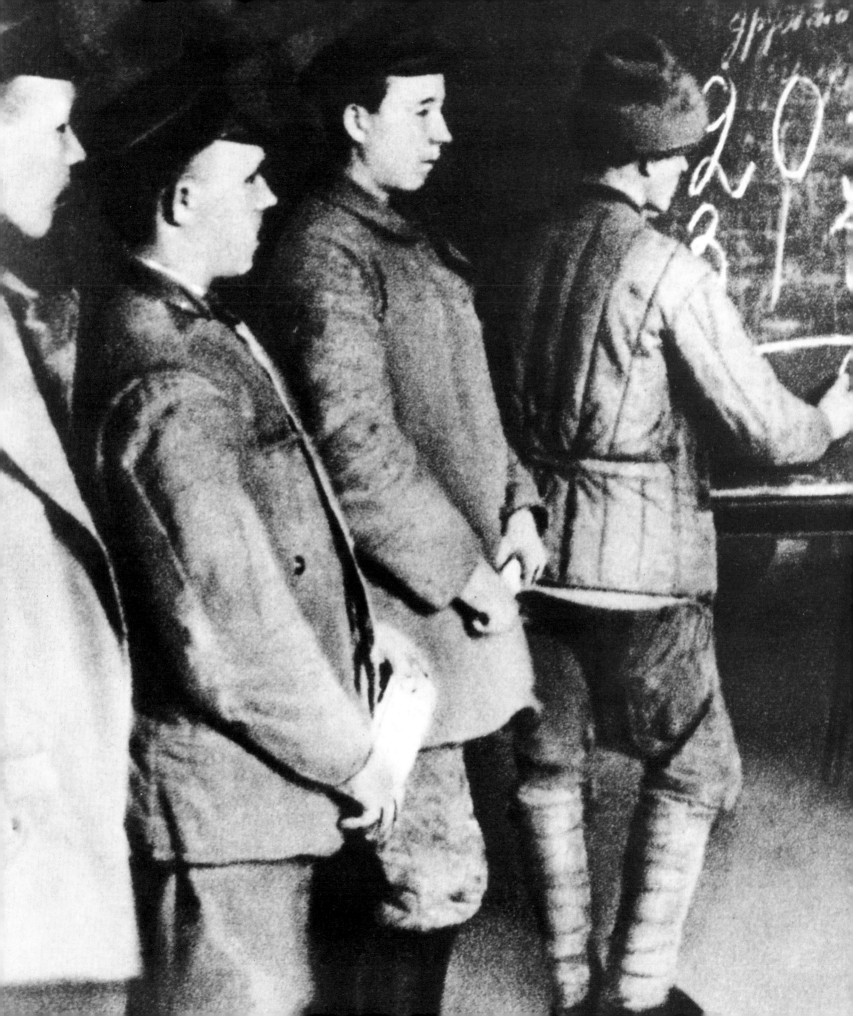

This work by a Yakut artist does not only tell of the great experience of "light" in a remote settlement of Eastern Siberia. It is at the same time an example of the original and inventive art of small nationalities in the Soviet family of peoples. The special attraction of this art is its care for artistic tradition, and close relation to folk art.

"Light", linocut by V. Vasilev

and put together the damaged machines. Towards the end of 1924 they achieved their aim, and the production of the factory greatly increased through the women's determined action.

The knowledge that they were useful to society as a whole was the most important element in the new self-confidence of women workers. Liberation of woman was therefore never regarded as a mere intellectual concept in the Soviet Union, nor founded primarily on the extension of woman's education, important as that might be. It was paramount that woman should take part in the building up of the country, and become involved in running it. To achieve this, woman had to be freed from domestic slavery, to create proper conditions for her working life. During the time of the hardest struggle, children's homes, nurseries and crèches were opened. Under the motto, "Everything for the child", children were saved from hunger and cold, and conditions created for woman's emancipation. In spite of all this, it never proved easy for women to find their new role in society, and even with the greatest efforts complete integration of women into the rebuilding of society was not achieved immediately. Indeed, the number of women workers declined during the first years of rebuilding, as industry, still underdeveloped, was able to draw its labor force in many regions from fully qualified male workers who had either returned from the front or were streaming into industry from the countryside. This decline in female labor meant a slackening in the development of equality between the sexes, and was contrary to government policy. Under Lenin's direction mea-

sures were taken to deal with the situation, limiting at least the decrease in female labor, and also ameliorating the hardships experienced by women because of the lack of employment.

By the end of 1924 the worst was over, and the period of reconstructing the economy concluded. More and more women began to work, and in the two following years their numbers in industry multiplied more than eleven times. The work of women largely contributed to the fact that in 1926 the pre-war level of production was regained. This was, of course, the level of an industrially very underdeveloped country measured by world standards. For the working people of the Soviet Union, however, the rebuilding of the economy meant proving their strength and their ability to do great things. In a few years, mastering modern methods, they had by their own effort and under difficult conditions turned mountains of debris into an economy which in time would become the basis for a better life.

In the years to come women on many construction sites ceased to feel oppressed, ceased to feel second-rate beings, as they took their places alongside men. They adopted red kerchiefs as symbols of the country's progressive spirit, adding a touch of color to factories and building sites.

Fedor Gladkov's book *Cement* strikingly describes the process of woman's liberation in everyday working life and her changed ways of thought and action. Gladkov does not gloss over matters, and does not fail to relate in his tales those excesses which the enthusiastic acceptance of the new ways brought about. The fair-haired Dasha has her hair cut very short under her red kerchief, not because she thinks it attractive and easy, as we might nowadays, but because for her the haircut is a symbol. Other women in the cement factory copy her, and one of them explains at the women's meeting: "I cut my hair short, because you know yourselves how woman's long hair is the rope by which she is caught and then tied up like a beast."

These were also the years when many searched for new relationships between the sexes on the excuse that everything reminiscent of the old life was to be changed immediately and without transition. So it happened that marriages entered into quickly by many, particularly revolutionary women and men, were equally quickly dissolved. Indeed it must be recognized that many of the radical Left had wrong ideas about freedom in matters concerning sex. This may be explained by the uncertainties consequent on the changing of all values through the revolution, but it did not last, and by the 1930's such excesses were overcome.

Otherwise a largely underdeveloped country changed into a mighty industrial power under the eyes of the astonished world. Everywhere in the Soviet Union there rose new factories and power stations, rivers changed their course, and, above all, heavy industry developed as the "heart" of a new modern industry.

The decision to develop heavy industry first, thus attaining self-sufficiency in agricultural machinery, to say nothing of securing the national defense, meant that the people had to forego in the meantime many of the comforts of life. The Russian woman was less well dressed and had to choose in the shops from a smaller selection; she was also less well housed than working-class women in some countries of the West. But it must be realized that the masses of women workers and peasant women were kept in touch with big governmental decisions through congresses to which they sent their delegates who, in fact, greatly influenced decision making. In the factories the women, in groups of ten, chose delegates who represented their interests constantly at the large meetings and then brought back the results to be put into action. From 1922 to 1928 the number of women delegates rose ninefold to 830,700, so that, with each delegate representing ten women workers, the most important problems of more than eight million women were discussed. These mass discussions greatly helped millions of women to understand that heavy industry had to take priority over consumer goods and that temporarily they had to do without all but essentials. There existed at that time a small but much noticed number of Russian women who idealized their "doing without" status and built up a whole theory related to the "Proletkult". (28) They despised all jewelry, dressed excessively plainly and scorned lipstick and nail polish as "attributes of bourgeois femininity". This phenomenon in the life of Soviet women was a curious temporary aberration brought about by the immense and unsettling changes. At the same time thousands of women willingly took upon themselves the hardships of a rough pioneer life. They accepted the bitter cold of the Siberian north, the loneliness of the primeval forest, the war against myriads of mosquitoes, the fear of bears and wolves, in order to help in out-of-the-way places where new towns were being built, where wealth was to be obtained from

The socialist homeland is in danger. Work squads—men and women— march to the front. They are to relieve the wounded fighters, whose bent forms are seen on the bridge . . . The revolution cannot be beaten.

Aleksander A. Deineka.
The defense of Petrograd. 1927

Women have come to tea.
Maybe the hostess,
according to tradition,
has placed a bead of glass
into the dough,
or a coin.
For, it is said,
that she who finds it,
will meet with good fortune.

Smiling, the rite
is accepted,
knowing fully well,
that fortune
does not dwell in cakes.

the soil or the power of water transformed into electrical energy. This pioneer spirit, acquired in hard times, has been passed on by a generation of women to their daughters and granddaughters. Today, under much more favorable conditions, these younger women still help in opening up new territories. They have conquered the Siberian forests, tamed large rivers and helped to build new factories.

But in spite of the many and diverse efforts of a whole nation, the slogan "Everything for the child" has not lost importance. Generous protection for mother and child has been developed, schools have risen everywhere as well as modern nurseries and crèches. The misery of starving children is a haunting memory; and what could have tied mothers closer to the Soviet regime than the joy of witnessing a healthy, cheerful young generation, well trained in body and mind?

Before the revolution every third child died before reaching the age of three. There were even parts of the country where every second infant perished in his first year because of malnutrition or epidemic. But in 1930, when the Soviet Union was represented for the first time at a World Health Exhibition, the public learned that along with the basis of modern industry, an excellent health administration, second to none, had been created in Russia. From 1917 to 1927 the number of crèches increased twelve times. The number of nurseries rose one and a half times between 1924 and 1928. In 1929 when every rouble in the Soviet Union was needed mainly for the development of heavy industry, the state put aside more than one hundred million roubles from social insurance funds for the care of pregnant women, both pre-natal and at birth, and for care of the newborn child, as well as for the feeding of children in general.

Formerly, dreaded epidemics had spread from Russia into Western Europe, mainly typhoid and cholera. Many millions of Russian people had never set eyes on a doctor in all their lives. After a decade of socialist development the same country possessed a most up-to-date and effective medical service, among the best in the world. And all this was only a beginning. Today the health care of every citizen of the Soviet Union begins even before he is born, to end only with his death. All through life, regardless of cost, medical care is free.

This secure feeling about her own and her family's health is a contributing factor to the Russian woman's joyful and positive attitude to work. Another factor is the rising level of qualification of women. Gradually, unskilled labor has declined among working women. Women have conquered many trades and professions, remarkably so engineering, where women have never before played a part. From 1926 to 1931 the number of women locksmiths increased fourteen times, that of lathe operators seventeen times, and that of machinists twenty times. In these developments women had to stand up for themselves against the prejudices and the conservatism of many a manager, and against the deprecation of their qualifications by isolated opportunist trade union functionaries.

The striving of the Soviet woman towards equality was certainly not without problems. It was difficult, for example, not to let the women in marginal areas fall behind. In many regions there had never been any industry.

*The girl with the red kerchief
became the symbol
of the liberated self-confident
woman with equal rights,
in the first socialist country.*

Georgy Georgievich Ryazhsky.
The delegate. 1927

Vilem Andreevich Chekanyuk.
The first Komsomol cell in the village.
1958

In 1917 women weavers sent a few looms to Armenia, together with a note saying: "Take these as our modest contribution towards the building-up of your texile industry." When trying to win over the women of Central Asia and Transcaucasia to the merits of education, training and working outside the home, the Soviet government ran into serious difficulties. It was met by unrelenting hostility from feudal landlords. The situation was one of total absence of rights for women and their suppression in society and in the home. All the same, the number of women working in a trade or profession increased remarkably in the Central Asian Soviet Republics during the late 1920's. Statistics for the year 1926 show that altogether there were employed in the industry of Central Asia twelve women from Uzbekistan, one from Turkmenistan, and two from Tadzhikstan. In 1932 the silk industry alone accounted for 2,350 women workers of different nationalities in the Central Asian republics. In Uzbekistan the share of women working in industry rose from 12.3% in 1928 to 35% in 1935. In these regions, too, women became more skilled. Their qualifications approximated more and more closely to those of their male colleagues, an important condition for equality in economic life. The government took a number of measures to ensure education and continued training of women. It was then that the experience gained in the earlier fight against illiteracy in vast parts of the country came into its own.

As late as 1926 only 37.1% of all women in Russia could read and write, compared to 66.5% of men. Year by year, however, the relation changed in favor of women. This raising of the level of education allowed large numbers of women in formerly backward areas to do skilled work.

And how did women in the villages fare? Until 1928 living standards in the country were much lower than those of the towns. Scattered small holdings were worked with hardly any technical equipment, and were in sharp contrast to the country's industry. The economically stronger and bigger farmers, the kulaks, sabotaged any central authority. But in the early thirties when conditions were ripe, on the basis of modern industry, to create collective farms, the owners of many small and medium-size farms joined to form these collectives. For many it was a difficult decision, particularly for women, as it meant a complete change in the way of life and giving up age-old customs. It meant saying farewell to relative independence, precarious as this might have been. It is not surprising therefore that for many women the change necessitated much adjustment of their whole way of thinking, convincing themselves in the end that collective work and collective property would allow them and their children a life more worthy of human beings.

A peasant woman on a collective farm in the village of Borrissovka near Ufa vividly describes the change which took place in just one generation: "My late father never ate pure bread all his life long, and he did not know what "resting" meant. The lamp was seldom lit, there was no money for paraffin. We, women and girls, had to spin in the dark. If my father could see this village now, look into the houses and the barns, and could hear what the people talk about ... my father just could not grasp it. If he saw our trucks, the club, the

She has fulfilled
a long-standing desire
to see the treasures of the gallery.
Now she walks, stands still
and is amazed at the miracle
of so much color and beauty,
never guessing that she, too,
is a miracle,
an everyday "Russian miracle":
a peasant woman
from a distant village
now a guest of Titian, Rubens
and Repin.

*BAKU is the name of the picture
by the German painter Heinrich Vogeler.
He made it as a sketch for a poster,
with the enthusiasm of the proletarian
artist and internationalist,
depicting the victorious revolution.
His very special approach and technique
enabled him to represent a wealth
of impressions, telling the onlooker
how heavy industry became the basis
for the country's flourishing.
The picture tells of the many forms
of new life, new culture and,
again and again of woman, liberated.*

school, our car, and his grandchildren eating cabbage soup with meat and a lot of butter in their gruel, he would be amazed. He would be amazed to see the amount of wheat in our barns, the cow in the yard, the sheep, the goats, the pigs and the turkeys. He would not believe his eyes, wouldn't know where he was, and what had happened in this world."

In place of the miserable "black huts" with their poor smoky holes for chimneys, which also housed the beasts in winter to save them from the icy cold, there are now comfortable settlements. Very many peasant women who had learned to read and write took the next important step in their emancipation: they became experts of collective agriculture, animal breeders, trained farmers, drivers of tractors and general cultivators. When the Stakhanov movement encouraged increased production all over the Soviet Union, a Ukrainian tractor driver, Pasha Angelina, reorganized work in her group so successfully that each tractor multiplied its set work. With this she supplied a new and remarkable initiative for the whole of Russian agriculture.

Was the evil proverb of the hen not being a bird, and the woman not a human being, then totally forgotten? Not completely, as changes take a long time to penetrate, and customs, even bad ones, are hard to eliminate. In Russia as elsewhere woman's emancipation did meet with resistance. A great many novels deal with these problems. However, the proverb was no longer typical of the general view. Even though the government was still a long way from the aims it had set itself and living standards were still modest, measured by today's norm, life had become worth living.

Increased production had increased the wealth of a whole society. The national income had multiplied by five, and the state could in the late thirties spend a great deal more on social services when women and children were the main beneficiaries.

In 1937 the number of women who could spend their vacation in a holiday home run by the public social services—compared to 1928—had risen by 500% and those being cared for in a sanatorium by 850%. All larger factories now ran crèches and nurseries, and the state decreed that parents had to pay only a quarter or at most a third of the expense incurred through the stay of their children in these institutions.

Much money was spent, too, on education, schools, houses of culture, and clubs which promoted sports and improvement of the people's health.

Dmitry Sveshnikov.
Portrait of a Siberian
woman teacher. 1960

Leonid Gershevich
Krivitsky.
Enthusiasts of the first
five-year plans. 1961

WORKER AND WOMAN
FROM A COLLECTIVE FARM

by Vera Ignatieva Mukhina—
a climax in the work
of a great artist.
The sculpture was made in 1937
for the World Exhibition in Paris.
All over the globe
it became the symbol
of the victorious revolution,
the building up of a new world,
and also of the
equality of the sexes.

Scorched Earth

On June 22nd, 1941 Hitler's Germany started war with the Soviet Union, and the country was immediately in serious danger, its two hundred million people facing a hard test of endurance. Quite apart from the role taken in its defense by men, never before in the history of mankind was there an example of such a massive and heroic involvement of women as in the years of this war, which the Soviet people have called the Great War for the Homeland.

The front was everywhere.

To all the efforts of women in production, in collective villages and in active service, there was added the grief over the death of husbands and sons, and the constant worry about relatives in the occupied zones.

Letters from women working in a Moscow brake factory to colleagues at the front show their sense of responsibility and the will to sacrifice: "For us no front exists and no country behind the lines. We shall use all our strength and all our energy to replace you in production, and supply you with everything necessary. We shall work day and night if required, and if necessary we will fight at your side."

Many Russian women fought in the ranks of the army. Marcjanna Fornalska, who with her children had gone to a remote village to work there in the collective, wrote in her memoirs: "News from the front was not good. Help was needed. But where was it to come from when there were practically only women left? It was not long before women here and there applied for permission to go to the front."

Women in the battles of a murderous war? This was no time for considering whether women would physically and mentally stand up to the hardships. An enemy, heavily armed, and used to victory, was devastating the homeland, destroying the fruits of years of the labors of construction, threatening even the very existence of the country itself. There certainly was no time for contemplation of whether figthing in the front line was harmful to woman's psyche.

A group of young women gliders—gliding had become popular with girls in the happy thirties—went during the first days of the war to the heads of the Youth League, asking to be sent to the front as pilots. They were discouraged by the authorities, anxious to save them from the pressures of such tasks. But the women persevered, training as night pilots, and learning to handle arms. They then formed the nucleus of an air division, consisting of women only, the 46th Women's Guard Regiment of Light Bombers. Night after night they flew through searchlights and anti-aircraft fire, struggling bravely against the enemy's fighters.

Many young women gave their lives in these fights. But not all were unlucky; their commander, earlier a well-known sports pilot, flew more than eight hundred sorties.

In a large part of the Soviet Union where eighty-eight million people lived before the war, the enemy had established a regime of terror. Hundreds and thousands of people, mostly women, children and the old, were horribly killed. Millions were deported in forced labor battalions to Germany, but in spite of all this a mighty resistance movement grew up.

Following double page:

Vladimir Dimitrov-Maistora. Everything for the front, everything for victory. 1945

Mikhail Savitsky. Madonna of the partisans. 1967

WAIT FOR ME

Wait for me, for I will return,
But wait anxiously.
Wait when the rain falls,
grey, dark and heavily.
Wait when the blizzard rages,
or summer glows.

Wait when the others have long
ceased waiting.
Wait when no letter reaches you
from places far away.
Wait, till nothing on this earth
is like your waiting.
Wait for me, for I will return,

I will, defying death,
which threatens me by day and night,
a hundred, yes a thousandfold.
Fighting for my country's freedom,
in the noise of battle,
in the midst of fighting I feel
protected by your waiting.

Konstantin Simonov

In Byelorussia 360,000 people fought in partisan units and 220,000 in the Ukraine.

There are no reports of the period telling of the number of women belonging to these units who in daring exploits entered the country behind the enemy lines, blew up railway bridges and installations, freed soldiers of the Red Army who had become prisoners, destroyed depots and whole enemy garrisons in towns and villages. Others supported the partisans with provisions, supplied them with ammunition, warned them of danger, and carried important messages. Their courage, and that of the very young and the old, made the partisan movement invincible.

A symbol for this invincibility was the struggle and death of the Young Guard, a group of nearly a hundred members of the Communist Youth League (Komsomol) from the industrial town of Krasnodon. Many of them were very young, almost children. To their vanguard belonged twenty girls, among them Ulyana Gromova, the "Ulya" Alexander Fadeev has described lovingly in his book, *The Young Guard*. She was a cheerful girl, he says, pretty, with plaits of thick dark hair and beautiful dark eyes. After many daring and successful actions against the occupying enemy, Ulyana and all her friends were captured and after brutal torture, laid down their lives. "Late at night two German soldiers carried Ulya into her cell, her pale face falling back and her long plaits sweeping the floor. They threw her down near the wall ... Lilya, who could hardly move herself, but tried to care for her friends to the last moment, rolled up carefully the bloodstained sleeves of Ulya's blouse. Shuddering with horror, she began to sob. There, on Ulya's back glowed a Soviet Star, still bleeding ... In the cells they could hear the mighty rumbling alongside the Don, and Ulya, trying to sit up, pressed her head against the wall, knocked and called: "Listen, boys, listen ... be strong ... our comrades are coming, our comrades are coming, in spite of everything."

Halina Chrostowska-Piotrowicz. Alone. 1959

In this land the enemy
may not trust even a hare's traces
nor where the hooves of oxen went,
nor the sound of harvest songs,
or the hammering of the
timberman's axe in the forest.
Everything is full of secret signals,
even the women's lullabies.

Desanka Maksimovic

Viktor Koretsky.
Cradle of the partisans. 1961

The girl Zoya Kosmodemyanskaya is also to be remembered. A pupil at a Moscow school, she joined the partisans and was taken prisoner by a German soldier while on a difficult mission. Bravely, she endured heavy torture, but never gave away one of her comrades. She was hanged at the age of eighteen. Another heroine was Pasha Savelyeva who died at the same age burned to death because an interpreter in an enemy headquarters she had at the same time spied for the partisans. But many pages could be filled recounting the heroism of Soviet women. Ulya, Lilya, Zoya, Pasha, their names stand for the valor of millions. They stand also for those women in the working collectives who gave everything they possessed, everything their families had saved, to get together the money for a single tank. Then there were those who learned to use the tank, and in it drove to the front. In the first difficult year of the war a mass movement had sprung up spontaneously amongst women to help the war effort in every way they could.

Notable even in such company were the women of Leningrad who set an example for all time, when during the months of siege they kept life going in that city, constantly exposed to attacks from the air and the fire from enemy guns. Struck down with grief over the many who perished with hunger and cold, the survivors kept moving debris, nursing the wounded, fighting fires, rescuing people from the ruins, comforting orphaned children, and working in the factories far beyond their bodily strength. In fact, the women of Leningrad were the hope of the besieged city. The defenses outside and inside the city were practically all the work

of exhausted, starving and freezing women, ready for any sacrifice. Another city whose women became famous was Moscow. Here the women turned their hands to everything from building defenses to manning them with anti-tank guns.

The murderous war lasted for nearly four years. When at long last it was finished in May 1945, much sadness was mixed with the joy of victory. Mothers wept for sons and daughters, children for parents, widows for their husbands and men for wives and children. A whole people mourned for millions of dead. The war had left 1,710 towns destroyed, 70,000 villages burned out, 232,000 factories wrecked, together with endless hospitals, schools, theaters and other buildings of a cultural nature.

They all waited for active creative people to rebuild them. The men returning from the front found their womenfolk matured, full of confidence in their own strength gained through experience.

Liberation

One of the most important results of victory over fascism was the founding of the People's Republics of central and southeast Europe. With the general change in these countries, there went also a basic change in the position of women. The process of obtaining equality of the sexes began at once in Poland, Czechoslovakia, Bulgaria, Hungary, Albania, Rumania, Yugoslavia and the then Soviet-occupied zone of Germany. It was in line with the new social system, and the leading part was played by a working class which always stood for the liberation of women from all oppression and discrimination.

That the process of this liberation was relatively quick was to a large extent due to progressive women in the countries themselves. They had fought at the side of men against the common enemy, and their heroic behavior in hard times left no room for male prejudice. These women had grown in stature and had the confidence and many of the essential qualities to accelerate the democratic process and the building up of socialism.

With so much to choose from it is difficult to pick only a few examples of women's part in the struggle for liberation from fascism.

In the ranks of the Polish army for instance there was a unique formation, "Emilia Plater", which consisted of 20,000 Polish women, many of whom had marched shoulder to shoulder with the Soviet army, from Lenino to Berlin, sharing its hardships, danger and sacrifices.

In Yugoslavia there were 100,000 women partisans on active service, while others did dangerous work in occupied towns and villages. They enrolled new partisan fighters, helped illegal fighters into hiding, obtained food, clothing and shoes, and saved the wounded. The women of Bulgaria, Rumania and Czechoslovakia shared equally bravely in the fight, many of them dying for the freedom of their country. Krystina Vituska in Poland, Jozefa Fajmanova in Czechoslovakia, a German woman, Katja Niederkirchner, Vela Peeva in Bulgaria, and Donca Simu in Rumania, these are just a few of the many who fought for freedom. Many books tell of the part women played in the resistance against fascism and war. There are songs such as the one about Vela Peeva who, wounded and exhausted, entrenched herself behind a rock, and fought against a superior force of police to the last bullet which she used to shoot herself. There is Donca Simu's lullaby for her child, a striking example that extreme bravery can go with tender femininity.

The women fighters who survived played a prominent part in the rebuilding of their countries. The beginning was hard, but the same fighting spirit that existed in the trenches and in the partisan corps conquered all difficulties. Marcjanna Fornalska describes on the last page of her memoirs her much longed-for return to the liberated city of Warsaw where she hoped to find her youngest daughter: "I now knew what it meant when people said that Warsaw was in ruins. I knew that I should never see my daughter again. The fascists had murdered her secretly, and we do not even know her grave."

"My tears kept streaming as my thoughts lingered over the ruins, and then, suddenly, I pulled myself together. There are thousands of mothers mourning, thousands who do not know the graves of their children. I do not just cry for my own children of whom one rests here under the ruins, and the other was perhaps gassed in the ovens. No, I grieve also for your children. There is one comfort only: never again that nightmare, never again war!"

Everywhere women did a great deal to overcome the misery of war. Their first concern was the children, their own, to secure for them at least a minimum of food and clothing, and then all the other children, uprooted by the war, and roaming in the countryside without parents and without a home.

Ruins were another thing to tackle, mountains of debris. Women had to break stones, haul wheelbarrows, slave at back-breaking tasks: young and old, girls and grandmothers, all were part of the scene in the cities returning to life. "Debris woman" was for many the first occupation, the first working relationship with others. Paintings and sculptures, stories and poems enshrine the memory of the "debris woman", that woman covered in dust, still suffering, yet glimpsing some hope in the midst of starvation and vast deserts of rubble.

Democratic reforms changed life in town and country. The people became the owners of real estate, factories and mines. Young working-class people and peasants set out to study at universities and technical high schools. Women were active in all this progress, barely aware of the fact that they were involved in a historic process of world-wide proportions. Many at that time did not think about a future in a socialist society. "Life can't remain as it is, and as neither God nor a supreme ruler can help us now, we must work, work and work again, and rebuild." That was the simple philosophy of millions.

In all countries freed from fascism the government of the people issued, immediately after victory, laws demolishing women's inequality. In all these countries women had, by and large, been kept down traditionally, considered second-class citizens only. In many parts of Hungary, Rumania and Yugoslavia the woman had humbly to stand behind the man when he sat eating. She had to walk behind him, eyes cast down, and be silent when matters other than domestic were discussed. It had been the same for centuries, and now—like the Dasha of Gladkov's novel *Cement*—there came these never resting communist women who didn't even seem to take time off to sleep, inviting women to political meetings, and assuring them of their equality with men. This, the women said, must be used positively. They must shape their destiny, vote and be voted for. And they must learn, study, and become educated.

Once again the old truth was confirmed that man's way of thinking changes much more slowly than the circumstances of the society he lives in.

A simple poem from Poland which Edward Fiszer wrote for one of these active women, Ruzena, reflects, half smiling, half in earnest, some of the strains encountered by progressive women in the early days of their emancipation:

Don't look so gloomy, Ruzena,
Your cares are ours, you are not alone.
Are people difficult? Don't care too
much, Ruzena—in time they will wake up.

There was still a great deal of illiteracy in many regions. In the villages of Rumania only very few people could read and write. In Bulgaria 27% of the people were illiterate, 23% in Poland, and everywhere more women than men. Without education there could be no progress, and things took shape according to the pattern of the Soviet Union. Adults thronged to the schools, taking pains to read and write, slowly and with care, letter after letter. It took only a few years to almost wipe out illiteracy, and this meant to thousands of women the first step on the road to a career, a career which had been firmly barred to them before.

The situation was somewhat different in the then Soviet-occupied zone of Germany. The task of drawing women into active participation for a democratic rebuilding of the country was more difficult there than in other countries. Twelve years of fascism had undermined the class-consciousness of a large section of male and female workers, with a loss of their democratic tradition. Clara Zetkin's appeal, shortly before her death, had gone practically unheeded: "Working women! Remember that fascism takes away your rights, rights you have obtained for yourselves in a bitter struggle ... Remember, that the Third Reich wants to degrade you to be man's slave and a machine for bearing children. Don't forget the courageous women, the fighters whom fascism holds in its prisons." Many of the heroes of the resistance saved the honor of the German working class. Among them were women of whom the writer Anna Seghers said: "They are our mothers and sisters. You would not now be free to learn or to play, indeed you might not have been born if these women had not put their delicate tender bodies like shields of steel before you and your future, all through the terror of fascism."

The women fighters against the Hitler regime who went through hell and survived became active the moment they were free, proving themselves wherever they were placed. They sat on women's councils, and cared for the wretched women of Germany, showing them the way to a new and better democratic country. From the beginning there sat together on these councils communists, social democrats, women not belonging to any party and members of the old bourgeois women's organizations. They put into effect a democratic coalition, such as appeared desirable in all spheres of public life.

In 1946 the vast majority of able-bodied workers were women, three fifths, in fact, of all able to work: a direct result of the terrible war casualties. Not many took an interest in politics; they had had quite enough of it. But on one point they all agreed with those who started political discussions again and again to win them over, and this one point was: never again war. The passionate rejection of war, born out of misery, suffering and bitter experience, brought many German women under the influence of progressive forces, let them overcome their lethargy and fight for peace.

In August 1946 the Soviet occupying forces issued an order concerning equal pay for equal work. Before 1933 generations of German women workers had carried this demand into the streets yet its realization was not well received by many. Not only men but women too aired the old argument that, after all, man

"Romance", pen and ink drawing from the cycle "Volgograd" by Erhard Grossmann

was the main breadwinner of a family, and he should therefore earn more. Also, woman's working strength had always been considered inferior as had been her performance, and she had been paid accordingly. However, this Soviet order did become the first and decisive step towards complete equality of women in East Germany.

In those days there was much discussion, particularly among young people, coming to terms with the past, about how to understand the new order which they were helping to bring into being. In the youth organizations there was then growing up that generation of girls who now—as mature women—can be found in responsible positions in the economic, cultural and political life of all socialist countries. Even though there was much discussion in the early days after the war, time was not wasted in mere talk. There was a great deal of hard work, and tremendous achievements in industry and agriculture, and among the pioneering workers were many women. A German poet, Kuba, a pen-name for Kurt Bartel, wrote a poem which describes the situation of those years:

They will say of our days:
Rubble there was and little courage.
For low was their strength after defeat.
And the blood ran bitter in their veins,
As they clung to life in its worn-out track.
They will say.
One day they will stand on terraces made
  of glass,
Point to bridges,
And to gardens,
And at their feet will be the new town.

And they will say:
Those who laid the foundation stone,
Were laughed at; they were starving,
And yet
They planned, they built, and they moved
Stones from the rubble.
When they thought about their work,
They cursed.
Yes,
They doubted their own strength.
They had inherited curses;
War and treason confused their minds.
But from the ruins grew strength
Grew building up.
And the building was a new beginning.

In May 1947 an association of German democratic women was founded which carried on the best traditions of the earlier German women's movement and united members from all strata of society, independent of individual views. This association was to play an important part in helping women to adjust to new concepts. It coped bravely with the needs of the moment, particularly those of the old and the very young. The work of these devoted women also contributed greatly towards creating confidence again in things German all over the world. Distrust quite naturally existed after the horrors of the Hitler regime, even among organizations of women in other countries. This distrust can be understood all the better, if one remembers that in the women's concentration camp at Ravensbrück alone 92,000 women from eighteen nations were murdered.

Yet the Soviet and Polish women who had suffered most under the Hitler terror readily advocated the inclusion of the women's organi-

zations of East Germany into the Women's International Democratic Federation. This was actually agreed upon at the world congress in Budapest in December 1948. By now women in East Germany had left their pa. behind and gone a good part of the road towaı Js democracy and socialism. They had joined the ranks of women fighting for a lasting peace, taking this path at the side of progressive men, and in no socialist country was the fight for equality a fight against men. Much help was received from the women of Russia who had taken upon themselves trouble and sacrifice to assist in the rebuilding of their own country, and to meet the economic aims of post-war planning. Yet, they were ready to help wherever help in word or deed was needed. They knew from experience every step on the thorny path to emancipation.

Valuable friendships developed in that way.

In 1949 when the Soviet-occupied zone of Germany became the German Democratic Republic (GDR), it, like other socialist countries, decreed in its laws full equality of the sexes in all spheres of life, thus solving the question of woman's status once and for all. The constitutional provisions concerning this are very similar in Poland, Rumania, Czechoslovakia and the German Democratic Republic, so that it will suffice to quote examples from the constitution of the GDR:

Article 6
All citizens have equal rights.

Article 7
Men and women have equal rights.
All laws and decrees contrary to woman's equality are repealed.

Article 18

Men and women, adults and youths, have the right to receive the same pay for the same work. Woman enjoys special protection in the working relationship. The law of the republic will create institutions to guarantee that woman can combine her task as a citizen and creative person with her duties as wife and mother.

Article 30

Marriage and family are the foundation of community life. They enjoy the protection of the state.

Laws and decrees which impair the equality of man and woman in the family are repealed.

Article 32

During childbearing and while rearing children woman has the right to special protection and care of the state.

The republic will publish a law regarding the protection of mothers. Institutions for the protection of mother and child are to be created.

Article 35

Every citizen has an equal right to education and the free choice of a career.

As we have said before, it is not enough to have rights; it is equally important to make full use of them.

We shall now investigate how far equality for women has become a reality in socialist countries. How do women live there? What part do they play in industry, in the family and in public life? What are their joys and their problems? What has equality done for them? Has it added anything to their femininity, their charm, and their ability to love?

Future from the Beginning

Visitors to socialist countries are often anxious to know how the truly emancipated generation of women in these countries has realized its interests and ambitions. This question is answered easily in August Bebel's words, which in his days were a vision only: "Woman's education is equal to that of man."

And when does this process of equal education begin, when does actual equality begin in the life of woman? The answer is: on the first day of her life or perhaps even earlier in the minds of the two people expecting a child.

For many centuries it has been the acknowledged desire of men to beget a son. Therefore women who did not bear sons had to suffer. It is logical that the cult of "the son and heir" should disappear in the new socialist views on property and the new position of woman in socialist society. Questionnaires have shown clearly that most couples have adjusted to these new ideas, though some young women are still anxious to bear a son. More often than not this wish goes back to the subconscious longing to see their husband and lover reflected in their child. If a family name is considered important by some people, it can now be handed on by a daughter in many socialist countries. A couple can choose to adopt the woman's family name, a possibility not made use of very often so far.

In all socialist countries the birth of a girl is announced with equal joy to that of a boy, but it would still be wishful thinking to believe that the education of small girls is yet on an equal footing with that of boys everywhere.

In the German Democratic Republic the *Zentralstelle für Hygiene des Jugend- und Kindes-alters* has investigated this problem under the guidance of Professor Schmidt-Kohner, a well-known woman sociologist. This investigation shows the difference of performance in a sample of 540 children aged four to six.

It was established that overall there was no basic difference between boys and girls, and they were equally developed intellectually. It is interesting, however, to learn that there were some significant differences in dealing with "concepts". "Vehicles" received better responses from boys, while "vegetables" fared better with girls. Girls at five or six years of age were also better when it came to knotting a thread, tying ribbon, and making a bow. The investigators do not doubt that these differences are due to an outmoded way of training according to sex. In her book, *The Feminine Mystique*, the American psychologist Betty Friedan pointed to the one-sided training of girls in the homes of the United States which is orientated towards marriage and motherhood as the only aims in life. As a basic conception of the past, it has not been completely superseded even in socialist countries. So long as these patterns vary with girls and boys in the early years of childhood, the old idea about "woman's place" will linger. It will linger as long as the family supports only "typically feminine" kinds of play, and then sets "typically feminine" tasks later on. Girls with that kind of background, and likewise boys treated accordingly, will have the wrong approach to the other sex, and will display a lack of variety of interests at

When, after the war, Wolfgang Borchert proclaimed to the world all his despair at the wasted hopes of a young life shattered and disrupted, he spoke of a generation without time to take leave, without ties, depth, good fortune or home. Yet, he did not doubt that a new beginning was dawning. We are, he said, a generation full of new beginnings, beginnings on a new planet, beginning a new life with a new sun, and new in heart. There will be new love and new laughter.

The head of a Siberian nursery,
when asked why the children fitted
so cheerfully into their small community,
replied: "We speak to them softly . . ."

Young ones in a train
which takes them into the future.
Time flies past.
But for the young ones in the train,
it goes much too slowly.
They would like to get out,
run in front of the train
and into the future.

Louis Fürnberg

A great longing
has come about
to discover
the causes of all things.

Bertolt Brecht

Just a symbol in a plan,
means ten thousand people, their
hearts beating warm and joyfully.
Or sunshine on the faces of children.
It may mean transmissions,

rousing songs, fields of waving corn
and bales of cloth,
locomotives and ships.
Mock less at the files of today.
Louis Fürnberg

Rumyana Gancheva. On the way to practical work

school. With boys directed towards mechanical matters, building, playing with cars, tractors and locomotives and the early use of tools, their interest in these things is wider from the start, leaving girls handicapped on that scale. However, one-sided training according to sex is certainly on the wane, and the most important cause for its disappearance is the attitude cf working parents and the steadily growing influence of nursery education.

The crèches, deliberately and on the basis of modern educational experience, see to it that all children receive the same stimulation for "conquering" their surroundings, according to age. In the nurseries of all socialist countries there are as many daring girl astronauts as there are boys enthusiastic to enter outer space. There are also good "fathers" bathing dolls and feeding teddy bears side by side with little girls caring for their dolls. Toys which further technical sense, precision and creative thought fascinate girls as much as boys, while boys like making chains of glass beads as much as do girls.

Publicity in all socialist countries has contributed much to changing the emphasis in education. Courses for parents, public lectures and popular discussions in the mass media, as well as an extensive literature on the subject, clearly show the growing trend for giving children the same chances for the basic development of their abilities irrespective of sex.

This principle does not mean that man and woman are the same, but it does mean the striving to abolish one-sidedness and inequality of opportunity which in the past hindered girls in particular from fully expanding their personality.

Life at school is, ot course, tuned to education for equality. There are differences in the educational systems of socialist countries due to varying conditions and assumptions. But everywhere schools recognize their duties towards realizing the right, laid down in the countries' constitutions, of equal education for all. And this is no longer an ideal to be aimed at, but rather an accomplishment largely achieved. Nobody is now handicapped by lack of money or social position in obtaining the education he or she is capable of accepting. Nowhere are there now the once typical one-room schools for underprivileged village children.

In this kind of education girls achieve the same as boys. They no longer lag behind in science. They prove their logic in math competitions, and their ability to think in abstract terms. If demanded and encouraged these qualities belong to girls as much as to boys and polytechnic education is a further step in the diversified training of girls. (29) Polytechnic colleges mean practical training, spanning the ancient gap between school and life. Education here is angled towards training the abilities of every student for work in a particular industry. Girls and boys become acquainted with the theory and practice as well as with the basic scientific principles of production. This is done in conventional subjects, natural history and mathematics, but also in specially arranged classes.

Gabriele, one of the girls in our questionnaire, may serve as an example. In her seventh year at school she had three new subjects in her program: a full day of instruction in production, an introduction to socialist industry and a course in technical drawing. From then on Gabriele went once a week to a state-owned factory (nearly all larger industrial and agricultural enterprises have up-to-date departments for the training of students, a students' workshop or polytechnic centers). Here Gabriele learned to work under expert guidance according to her physical and mental capacity. The training of her manual skills was important and so was the general broadening of knowledge and experience which Gabriele and her friends obtained in this way. Advantages for the factory were never a consideration. All the same, school and factory are concerned in that the pupils should do useful work and this training-working day is the nucleus of polytechnic education.

Her second subject, with the slightly complicated name of "introduction to socialist industry", gave Gabriele an insight into the many branches of mechanical technology, knowledge of machines, electro-technology, techniques of distribution, computer science and economics in general. In addition she was given an hour a week of technical drawing.

When, after ten years at school (30), Gabriele took leave of her teachers, she had—along with far-reaching dreams—both feet firmly on the ground. She could use her abilities adequately in practice and had acquired practical as well as abstract knowledge. And most important at the start of a career was her respect for physical as well as mental work.

She had experience of both. She knew the length of a working day and that the fulfillment of planning programs requires a person's individual attention. At the same time she realized that successful work makes for contentment.

At the end of her tenth year Gabriele did not just begin to look around for a career, in a way which might have led to rash decisions: she had been prepared over a long period of time for this step into the real world. Career decisions by boys and girls are usually made in the next to last year of school, and a well-designed system of training prepares them for this.

There is naturally in the life of every young person a time when superficialities might lead to random choice. Eight out of fourteen girls in Gabriele's class had wanted to become stewardesses, two had wanted to serve in the television tower and three to become hairdressers. But through a direct knowledge of factory work the girls saw their choice widening. They formed likes and dislikes, and they learned what kind of work had a future. Gabriele and her friends realized that the economy has more need for skilled technical workers and engineers than, for example, stewardesses, and that there are good prospects for girls with special skills.

In the last decisive months experts from various branches of industry come to the schools to advise, explaining in detail to parents and pupils the qualifications necessary, the tasks to be expected, the chances of advancement and the financial possibilities in various important careers. These experts also give individual advice when needed. Gabriele, for example, made her decision after discussing her abilities and her plans with parents, teachers and experts, before choosing to work in construction engineering. It was at this time that she enthusiastically answered the questionnaire about her expectations for the year two thousand.

At her school the teaching staff together with the parents had been particularly good in helping to guide the young in their search for a suitable career. In recent years psychologists, familiar with the problems of work and of the young, have been brought increasingly into vocational counselling. Their work can make a great contribution towards avoiding wrong decisions. There are, unfortunately, still schools which do not tackle the task either early or systematically enough, and their success is more limited when it comes to reconciling individual wishes and inclinations with the economic needs of the country.

In general, education at polytechnic colleges does prepare girls and boys for the transition to working life, giving them more confidence in themselves and helping them at the same time to plan their lives as a whole. The training gives girls the very same opportunities as boys for a varied and interesting career. Again to cite the German Democratic Republic: there are 306 types of vocational training available, and excluded from a girl's choice are only those that still require heavy physical work, or others with requirements unsuitable for a woman's physique.

It is, of course, acknowledged in the socialist countries too that the different physical attributes of man and woman demand differentiation in the work to be done. Some characteristics such as the relatively smaller physical strength of women and the facts of menstruation and childbirth, offer difficulties in careers which demand bodily strength. The lack of certain qualities is actually compensated by others which make woman superior to man in a number of jobs—perseverance, precision,

manual skill, etc. Naturally, equality does not mean being the same, and that goes for choosing a career. The degree of emancipation can only be measured by the job opportunities a woman is able to make use of. What is certain is that year after year the choice of careers for women is expanding, due partly to scientific and technological development which is eliminating more and more heavy work that is unsuitable for women.

Even with equality of opportunity, not all young people can become astronauts or atomic scientists. Under socialism as under any other system, people's physical and mental abilities vary, as well as their inclinations, talents and abilities. However, every young person should be able to exploit his or her own gifts to the fullest and use the chances offered by society. If a girl wishes to be a worker, a hairdresser, a saleswoman or a cook, she should be well trained for her chosen career and become skilled and conversant with the latest developments in her field. Socialist schooling sets great store by one fact, and trains young people to recognize it. This is that all knowledge acquired is only the basis for more knowledge. Knowledge of a subject is not the final goal of learning but a means of gathering further knowledge. The time in which knowledge becomes obsolete is constantly getting shorter as new discoveries in all spheres are being made. Anybody ceasing to learn will be left behind, whether he is a skilled worker or a scientist, a man or a woman.

Considering the development sketched out here—a girl's education from nursery to graduation—it is not astonishing to learn that in the German Democratic Republic 97 out of 100 girls train for a career, and that many young girls choose careers of a scientific or technical nature, which have become open to them only recently.

In 1970 in the German Democratic Republic the distribution of women apprentices was:

skilled workers in computer science
79%
skilled workers in electrical engineering
76%
skilled workers in chemical industry
67%
skilled workers in plastics industry
80%
skilled workers in general engineering
56%

Of course, and this is fortunate, the traditional careers for women are still attractive to many. Every society needs nurses, typists, hairdressers, saleswomen, kindergarten teachers, midwives, and even stewardesses.

The choice of a career for girls does not differ widely in other socialist countries, except for differences in degree where technological careers are concerned, according to varying economic situations. To people in socialist countries it appears puzzling that in a highly industrialized country, such as France, 48% of all young people, mainly girls, work in unskilled jobs after leaving elementary school.

The victory of a new ideal in education can nowhere come about automatically, and even less so if it means a complete change of values concerning the role of woman in society. New standards are acquired only in constant con-frontation with the traditional set of values, and this is a much slower process than mere economic changes.

Thus some girls have to face contradictions between their home upbringing and their education at school.

In all socialist countries there are likely to be girls more strongly influenced by their backward upbringing at home than by their progressive schooling. The plan for their lives often does not go beyond marriage, and they are far removed from the bustle of their more up-to-date contemporaries. It must be said, however, that the number of girls preparing for their part as housewife only, leaving aside all other chances, is becoming smaller and smaller. Under the circumstances it is not strange that girls who do not train, and look for nothing but a husband, run the risk of becoming less and less popular.

The ideas of man about the "ideal woman" have greatly changed, actually from the nursery upwards, through boys mixing with girls on terms of equality, common education and equal opportunities. Equality in education makes quite naturally for higher demands in the partner.

Saying Yes to a Career

We can think with gratitude of that generation of women whose education was not yet equal to that of man, but who in difficult times confidently prepared the path today's generation is taking.

Let the facts speak for themselves. In the Soviet Union every second person with a career is a woman. In Poland the number of women with a career, compared to pre-war figures, has trebled; in Bulgaria it has risen from 381,996 in 1956 to 1,264,878 in 1971. Forty-seven per cent of the Rumanian and forty-five per cent of the Czech labor force are women. In Yugoslavia there are four million women working; 59.1% of all workers in shoe manufacturing and 37.6% in electronics are women. Two thirds of all Hungarian women now work in industry and agriculture. In the German Democratic Republic out of ten women of suitable age eight are working.

And what is the reason for eight out of ten women to go out to work, even though a career is often difficult to reconcile with family commitments, in a socialist society, too? In no socialist country is there a law compelling women to work at a job. The constitution guarantees them a job corresponding to their ability, equal pay for equal work, the right to take part in decisions and the shaping of the economic, political, social and cultural life, as well as the right to education. But there is no law to force women to use these rights.

Also, there is no discrimination against the woman who wishes solely to be a housewife. There are, indeed, thousands of women who

through looking after their children are tied to the house for years. But not to have a career without a good reason means, for a healthy and able woman, to have to swim against the tide.

All the same, it cannot be denied that remnants of traditional views on woman's destiny still linger. Woman finds herself in a conflict between the outmoded and the new.

Quite often the conflict is solved in favor of woman's traditional role. All this is, of course, a vestige from the days of inequality. Yet even in a socialist society the alternative still exists for many women. There are still women who have not quite forgotten the concept of a male breadwinner, believing that "by nature" man is meant to support the family.

Laws concerning the family in socialist countries do make it perfectly clear that both partners in a marriage are responsible for supporting the family, nevertheless it is still possible to live with the idea of man as the sole supporter. It is often quite comfortable! Socialism questions this as a path to permanent happiness and contentment. It maintains that there is something lacking in the life of the woman who cannot fully express herself and develop her individual personality. This woman may and often does object. The world turns, she will say to herself, and I am not in a position to make it turn any the quicker. In the socialist countries fewer and fewer women now relate their feeling of happiness and fulfillment to the private sphere only. Happiness to woman now means the development of her full potential. And this in turn means more than love, marriage and being a mother. It is realizing those talents and capabilities with which she is not less endowed than man. Yet, these abilities might not be discovered and would certainly not be encouraged without her becoming active in a career and in public life. Once discovered, they will contribute to personal happiness and to the common good.

How far have women in the socialist countries grasped these relationships and the interaction between personal happiness and service to the community?

In the Soviet Union, in Poland, in Czechoslovakia, the German Democratic Republic, Bulgaria and Hungary the results of sociological research concerning women's work motivation are available.

Naturally, in a socialist society as under any other system, a woman works because she wants to earn money, and in every country there are women, particularly those on their own, who have to earn money. The wish to earn money is by no means anti-socialist. After all, socialists are not pure ascetics, concerned only with the welfare of future generations. At the same time, their thinking is not ruled by consumer-pressures, and yet their daily work is important in that it determines the quality of life of their own family and the whole of society. That personal interests and endeavors can be in tune with those of society as a whole is one of the great advantages of the socialist system. Quality of life therefore, as understood by a socialist, does not just mean ideal values, such as freedom from exploitation, social security, education and equality; it means, equally, rising living standards for the individual. Heinz Kahlau, a poet in the German Democratic Republic, has expressed this thought with understanding humour:

> ... And mark my words:
> Each one should have his share.
> It's not enough to make descendants happy,
> So that they flourish when the ravens
> feast on us.

But at the same time Kahlau reminds his readers that they should not "sell out their dreams" for the good life:

> Don't give away your dreams nor daily
> bread.
> There's need for both in this short life
> of ours.

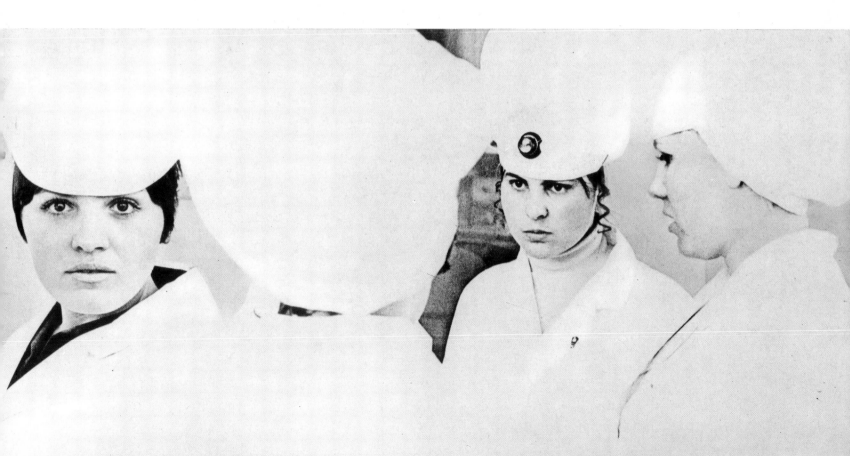

A. A. Dshafarov. A word about tomorrow. 1967

Wolfgang Mattheuer. Landscape at Bratsk. 1967

*At the magic center of crossroads
she stands inmidst the noise of motors,
stands Aphrodite,
or whatever her name may be.*

*She commands the elements,
rolling past her in waves,
gliding past the tangents
of her white arms.*

Wolfgang Jähnig

Issat Klychen. Masters of their trade. 1969   Viktor Petrovich Barvenko. The masters of Balkhar. 1961

Simple, clear-thinking people
like simple clear decisions.
Men of Good Will like simple things,
and simple, clear words.

Anna Seghers

Gisela May for the 50th stage anniversary
of the actress Helene Weigel:

She is a woman.
That may mean nothing.
Yet I venture to say that there are
certain qualities more marked
with us than with the other sex.
And she has these qualities.
All of them!

She is direct, attacking problems
in a straightforward way.
She is motherly,
strong in her feelings,
with a sense
for all that is beautiful.
She is reasonable.
She can get angry,
yet does not sulk.

She is a fighter
for the finest thing
in the world: peace.

Bert Heller. Prima ballerina Nora Mank. 1969
Gheorghe Anghel. Portrait of a woman. 1962

Once a foreign journalist,
looking at the Dresden
collection of paintings,
asked the price of the Sistine Madonna.
And the reply was another question:
"Do you know the price of the sun?"

Raphael's Sistine Madonna,
Titian's Christ of the Tribute Money,
Giorgone's Sleeping Venus
and many other precious masterpieces
might have been lost to the world ...
While still in the inferno of battle
people began to agitate about them,
and one in particular,
NATHALIE SOKOLOVA,
Soviet art historian, and then
major in the Soviet army,
helped to rescue the treasures
from final destruction in musty,
damp hide-outs.

In other words, to keep one's dream means not to live by bread alone, and to be able to rise above the mere earning of money.

The motive of wanting or even needing to earn money is becoming less and less decisive in choosing work and other motives are coming to the fore. Research by the Russian sociologists Khart'iev and Golod mentions the following psychological stimuli which go beyond financial considerations, in this order:

(1)
woman needs her own pay to secure her independence, equality with her husband and position in her family;

(2)
work makes for satisfaction and fulfillment;

(3)
the wish to be attached to a community;

(4)
develop one's own personality;

(5)
be useful to society.

With many of the women questioned some or all of these motives work together.

Other Soviet research, aiming at obtaining information regarding the concept "sense of life", shows that for the majority of women questioned, interesting, enjoyable work is, alongside a harmonious family, the essential assumption for leading a fulfilled life. It is not astonishing that the young generation, brought up and educated in socialist society, should express these motivations even more frequently and with greater force. The Polish sociologist R. Dionisyak put a question to senior-year pupils in a comprehensive school in Cracow: "What do you associate the idea of happiness with?" The overwhelming reply was: "Work one likes and family happiness." There was no difference in the replies of boys and girls.

How much congenial work influences thought and emotions can be seen with working women all over the world, particularly artists, writers and scientists. It is, however, specially obvious with the women of a socialist society.

We have already pointed out the causes of greater job satisfaction among the women of socialist countries, when we discussed the achievements of Soviet women during the rebuilding of their country in the 1920's and 30's. This same enthusiasm is maintained and even strengthened today under less trying conditions.

Equality and freedom to develop her personality to the full, thus mastering life, are the essential ingredients for woman's fulfillment in work.

Thinking Lights the Lamps of Life

Work satisfaction does not come from mere working. A type of work is required where man or woman can realize his or her true self and prove his or her worth at the same time. Marx in *Capital* quotes a saying by John Bellers, that work provides the oil for the lamp of life, while thinking lights it. Creative work presupposes thinking, the wish to learn and learning itself. For equality to become a genuine reality, therefore, does not just demand that a woman has a career; she must also be guided towards making the best possible use of her abilities and talents, and availing herself of all opportunities open to her.

Not surprisingly, Khart'iev's and Golod's research led them to the conclusion that the more qualified a woman worker is, the more satisfaction she gets from her work. Thus 81.1% of all skilled women workers in Kostroma, an industrial town in the heart of the European part of the Soviet Union, said that they were satisfied in their work, as compared with only 69.4% of the unskilled.

The Soviet Union is the most progressive country with regard to the development of careers for women. In decades of construction a great deal of valuable experience has been gained of which the other socialist countries reap the benefit. In the Soviet Union 40% of all scientists, 72% of all doctors and 71% of all teachers are women. Also, the so-called historic aversion of woman to technology has completely disappeared. Every third engineer in a country richest in the world in engineers is a woman, and the numbers increase every year. At the Moscow Institute for Energy the woman dean mentioned in a conversation the great number of female students. "Girls and the natural sciences, girls and technology ... no, that's not a problem ... 35% of the 14,500 students of the institute are women, and they prefer the most demanding and most complicated courses." In the new towns of Siberia, in the gigantic power stations, I have met many of these extremely well-trained women engineers. They were as enthusiastic about technology and science as about the great experience of pioneer life in Siberia.

In the Soviet Union, of course, prejudices have had time to vanish for about half a century. Mothers and even grandmothers of these remarkable girls had already become emancipated. They were the generation of the legendary builders of Magnitogorsk and Komsomolsk on the Amur, who laughed at the often repeated myth of the incompatibility of woman's mentality and modern technology, and they triumphed over it. One of my Siberian encounters seems worth relating in this context.

The illustrations to this chapter contain a photograph of a very young fair-haired woman, Lida Shumanova. From a training college for cooks she had come to the new town of Bratsk in the Siberian forests. Lida helped in the big kitchen looking after the energetic builders of the Angara power station. At that time her plans and ambitions did not go beyond being a good cook, a decent person and eventually a good mother. The power station and love changed Lida's dreams and her whole life. The intricate net of high voltage cables which lends new romance to the Siberian forests fascinated her. And soon enough there was somebody very willing to introduce pretty Lida to the secrets of electro-energy ... Volodya. The young man's parents were killed in the war, and he had come to Bratsk and studied electrical engineering in night classes. Under his influence Lida left the cooking pots to become an electro-mechanic. Now she is an electrical engineer responsible for repairs on the very transformers she had once marvelled at from a distance.

So too in countries which have not lived for so long under a socialist system, woman's role in the world of careers can no longer be compared to her former situation. Bulgaria may serve as an example.

In this formerly very backward country, where woman's progress in education was completely blocked, 45.7% of all experts with secondary and university education are now women. And that with women comprising only 43% of the working population. This actually means that in Bulgaria today there are more experts among a hundred working women than among a hundred men. Women make up 68.5% of all students at technical colleges and 51.6% of all university students. Also 59.3% of teachers, 41.7% of doctors and 58% of agronomists are women.

Twenty-five years ago there was not a single woman in the Bulgarian Academy of Sciences, apart from auxiliary staff. Today 35% of the scientific staff are women. Every fourth engineer in Bulgaria is a woman—25.4%—an astonishing development. Yet, in Bulgaria

I am going now to school
to learn the ABC
and suddenly it dawns on me
that only now I learn.

And now I read in books
and shyly spell out words,
and suddenly it dawns on me
that all I read is strange and new.

And now I'm learning algebra,
and I'm amazed to find
that all the sums I ever did
have never, never balanced.

And now I am studying history,
and my eyes are open wide
to see that all I knew before
was angled to impress.

And as I stand before the globe
the earth does speak to me;
when before it all was strange
and mute
as in ignorance I groped.

Louis Fürnberg

people say: "Every fourth engineer, well and good, but why only every fourth?" And this tremendous change in the life of Bulgarian women has happened in the lifespan of one generation. Behind the statistics lie much passion and perseverance in overcoming outmoded ideas, much willingness to learn, much sacrifice and hard work.

Statistics, from other socialist countries are equally impressive. In present-day Poland there are more fully trained female workers than male. Every second student of economics in Czechoslovakia is a woman, and at Rumanian universities now nine times more women become students than formerly.

Much has been achieved during the last few decades in the training of women, more than many would have believed when the difficult uphill struggle began. But nowhere in the socialist countries do people rest on their laurels. There are still too many women content to do unskilled labor, not yet able to overcome the obstacles in the way of full training. It would therefore be a half truth to report on

Erhard Grossmann. Studying at night. 1969

women in socialist society and count the outstanding successes only, without remembering the tensions inherent in all the opportunities socialism offers women for well balanced development. Tensions arise in personal and private life, and much effort is made to eliminate them gradually. It is particularly necessary further to improve the position of women workers in industry. Actually more than job satisfaction is involved here, important as that is in the life of the individual. And there remains much to be done to bring women's training completely in line with that of men. At the end of 1973 65% of all men in the German Democratic Republic and only 30% of women held the final certificate for skilled workers. However, this 30% (40% in agriculture) is a proud achievement when compared to the past, and even the present in other industrialized countries (France 12%, Luxemburg 4%, and the German Federal Republic 5%). (31)

Yet, further efforts are needed as lower skill for women still means lower pay, less knowledge of the process of production, and with the lack of this knowledge a much smaller chance of taking part in the democratic decision-making in industry.

The Soviet Union leads other countries with a model system of training for skilled women workers in industry and agriculture. There are a great many training facilities, including re-training and further training for a second career, for those women already experienced in some particular field. While taking further training courses women are exempt from work, but still receive full pay. There are also courses not requiring a break in work.

It can easily be understood that the training and re-training of women makes the best progress where the modernization of factories, and rationalization and automation of the processes of production make the biggest demands for up-to-date staff. As an example, work in the Soviet textile industry has changed so completely through the introduction of the most modern spinning and weaving techniques that some hundred thousand workers—mostly women in the textile industry—have to meet completely new requirements. In the Ivanov Worsted Combine and in many other Soviet factories, many methods for the further training of women have been evolved. The system of technical training begins with the exchange of practical experiences—discussions on the shop floor, followed by popular lectures about the demands of the technical revolution. In that way working women are brought up to date in their skills, and while their interest is stirred, they are encouraged to obtain further training.

In Bulgaria, too, in view of the quickly growing technical advances, and in an effort to realize fully woman's equality, women's training is a top priority, with or without a temporary break in work.

Late in 1972 a decree was issued in the German Democratic Republic concerning concrete provisions for the training of skilled women

This is Lida
who went to Siberia, to be a cook.
But, as she fell in love
with Volodya, an electrical engineer,
and also with the mighty
transformers, she left the kitchen
and the cooking pots,
studied and studied, and became
one of the many women engineers
in the Bratsk power station.

workers. This decree makes it a duty for state-owned industry and agricultural collectives to enter into a contract with women before training, listing all important training facilities, detailing duration of training, rules for supplying a person who looks after the results of training, leave from work, security of tenure, even with interruption of training through illness, pregnancy or family difficulties. Finally the contract guarantees a future place of work according to qualifications.

To carry through these far-reaching measures large sums are needed and complete involvement of the management of the industries concerned. In the first place, however, the measures need the complete involvement of the women themselves.

For people of the age of about thirty-five there now exists little difference in education between men and women, as both are placed equally at school, in the choice of a career and the training for it. In some socialist countries there is even a tendency for more young women than young men to obtain a degree from a university or technical high school. The problem for young women is, above all, to get work according to their qualifications and to go on studying in spite of their often heavy responsibilities to household and family.

But how do the forties and over fare?

We shall try to explain their situation on the example of a woman worker, fifty-four years old.

Born in 1921, the child of a working-class family, she had four brothers and sisters. Her father died when she was of school age, and the mother had to bring up the children on her own. Lieselotte, the "big girl", delivered newspapers before going to school. She was always tired, and her performance at school, in spite of a lively intelligence, was not particularly good. At the age of fourteen she had to go into a factory to earn money, and she never had the chance to train for a career. She married in 1939, had a daughter, and a son in 1941. That year her husband was killed in the war, and during a night of bombing the family lost their modest home. Two years of refuge with her children in a village followed, with heavy work on the land.

She returned to her destroyed home town in 1945, living in a roughly patched up place in a ruin. The family all but starved, while she worked as a debris woman for a year. Then the factory she used to work in resumed production. It was by now state-owned. She worked on metal-punching, and life slowly but steadily improved. Her children were growing up and doing well at school, getting to know things their mother had never dreamed of. The daughter became a skilled worker in electronics, and her son—after ten years at school—began training as a construction engineer. The mother, however, still worked at the punching machine. She had collected much experience in life and work which she generously shared with the younger generation. She lived for her factory and its success as part of her being, taking the factory's difficulties as personal worries. Her colleagues had made her shop-steward in their union, and told her a hundred times: "You should become a skilled worker; you've got the gifts to go on learning and get a master's certificate. You might even become head of the department." And why then did this woman not move ahead?

Ivan Kirkov. Woman in Red. 1961

Doris Kahane. Portrait of Dr. H. B. 1971

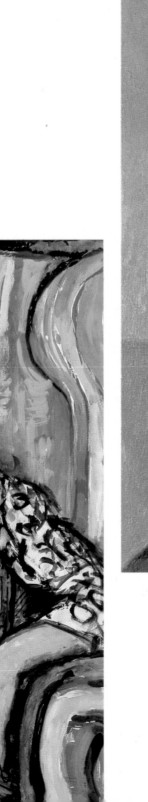

In one of the most famous libraries
of the world,
the *Lenin Library* at Moscow.
The young woman is called
Rinna Mineeva, candidate of science.

Her subject: magnetic resonance.
"My problem," she says,
"is enormous, without beginning or end.
A truly marvelous subject."

To be old, is not terrible,
said the Russian woman, reading.
She is still active, useful,
able to think even better
than in her young days,
give advice better
than in her young days,
read with leisure,
of which she has dreamed
for a lifetime.
She speaks with the wisdom
of a Sean O'Casey
who thought that ageing
was nothing but traversing
the crest of a mountain,
to descend to the other side of life
where new flowers grow,
and beauty abounds . . .
And the secret of "eternal youth",
said the reading woman,
is work.

Rosemarie and Werner Rataiczyk.
Woman studying. 1970—1972

Fear of responsibility? No, she would not mind greater responsibility, but she is afraid of studying, with too great an awe of "theory". "How could I keep up," she said, "with the young ones, with their sound education and their lively minds, and the way they can talk?"

All this makes her typical of many older women, afraid of the first step towards studying.

In all socialist countries where statistics are available, the readiness to obtain specialized training is greater with people of higher education. Women, as shown in our example, with only eight or even fewer years of elementary schooling naturally form the bigger proportion of unskilled workers.

The following table, concerning the relation of schooling to the readiness to obtain career training, was arrived at on the basis of surveys by the Ministry of Coal and Energy Production of the German Democratic Republic. It gives proof of the reluctance of women with less education to obtain vocational training.

Readiness to Obtain Specialized Training

	Yes	No	Not yet decided
8th year	20.6%	65.2%	14.2%
10th year	47.4%	26.3%	26.3%

Many thousands of women factory workers whose lack of schooling is a heritage of the backward past need help from society to overcome their disadvantage and be able to assume the place in production to which their long experience has fitted them. Their sense of responsibility and their personal relationship to their place of work, formed in the difficult years of reconstruction, make them particularly fit to take on bigger tasks.

At the end of 1973 an international congress at the Academy of Sciences in Berlin had as its subject: "The Training and Re-Training of Women in Industry."

On the basis of extensive research proposals were made which, if realized, would increase women's readiness for obtaining skilled training. It was stressed that the most important condition for this is the very recognition that such training is necessary. It is the knowledge of the concrete demands which the scientific and technical revolution and the shaping of the socialist society make on industry and its labor force. The generous conditions for education laid down in the 1972 decree must be matched by better measures at work to deal with women's special circumstances. Training must be arranged in such a way that women can cope with the heavier load of work and their domestic duties. Some experiences gathered have found a favorable response already in the German Democratic Republic, and have aroused interest in other socialist countries too.

For example, the state-owned Wolfen film factory, which employs many women, has adopted methods of skilled training which in contents and duration relate to the life and working experience of women. This lead five hundred women to obtain certificates of skill within two years. Another factory employing many women, the Esda Thalheim stocking combine, has obtained great success with similar measures, especially with its older workers. It is easily understood that these women will undertake further training more readily in the company of women of their own educational background. By 1980 two thousand women will have obtained skilled training within the firm's training program.

It is necessary to stress here that the object of all training measures is to create equal conditions for women to take their part in the progress of industry and the democratic life of the factory, and not to give them special privileges. Those women who are given better training facilities are fully aware of the fact that to obtain a certificate of skill demands hard work on their part. If standards of skilled training were to be lowered, it would in the end be to the disadvantage of women who would then be less well qualified than their male colleagues.

The drivers of electric streetcars in Berlin and Leipzig provide an interesting example.

For some time now these cars have run without conductors. The driver alone is responsible for the safety of the passengers. The drivers of the streetcars have always been men, while the conductors were women. What then was to happen to the women under the new scheme? There was persistent agitation among the women formerly employed as conductors to train as drivers, and the success was astonishing. Nearly all the women concerned obtained qualifications as streetcar mechanics as a precondition to becoming drivers. Now they are even better trained, more up-to-date than most of their male colleagues. And surely this additional training with all its problems and successes must have increased those women's confidence and job satisfaction. Most of the drivers in Berlin, when asked, replied that they enjoyed going to work, and that they would like to continue their work and their training.

This extra bonus of training, particularly with more mature women, should not be underestimated. The more a woman can achieve, the better the quality of her work, the more she feels she is needed in her place of work, the more recognition she receives, the less she is aware of getting older.

Extensive research in some large factories of the German Democratic Republic among women of comparable age groups, has found clear proof that, for example, problems associated with the menopause stand in direct relation to job satisfaction and recognition in work. It was shown that women in this age group who were in the thick of life, who were wanted and encouraged, contented in their community, confirmed and respected in their work, generally suffered less from "change of life" than women who at this time took account of their younger years and found that somewhere they had got stuck and had missed something important. Thus encouraging further training and correcting the shortcomings of earlier schooling serve many and different purposes. They help socialism attain its stated aim: to assist all people according to their abilities to develop their personalities to the fullest. For women they present a basis from which to achieve equality. Conforming with the demands which modern developments make on the worker, they create self-confidence, deepen job satisfaction, and for many women ameliorate the feeling of getting older.

Another facet of obtaining further training can best be expressed in the proverb: "*L'appétit vient en mangeant*". Experience shows that many women are ready to take the second step, dealing with increased responsibilities, once the difficult beginning has been mastered, and a certificate of skill has been won. The movement for further training will therefore contribute towards more women rising to higher and leading positions.

Much is done in all socialist countries to increase woman's participation in the higher ranks of the country's economy. And even what has been achieved so far goes beyond the part women play in these functions in the countries of the West.

We have mentioned already that every third engineer in the Soviet Union is a woman and every second school has a woman at its head—to repeat only a few examples. In Bulgaria the number of women engineers has multiplied by seven, and that of women technicians by eight. Women make up 14.2% of all factory managers and their assistants and 10.6% of the leading experts and their assistants. In Hungary the number of women in leading positions has risen by 35% in the last four years, and in construction engineering by 42%. All the same, even this high percentage is not enough, and socialist society everywhere seeks constantly to increase the number of women fit to take leading positions in industry and agriculture.

In principle there exists a great readiness to take on more responsibility, the greater, of course, the more confident and the more able women are.

Quite a few women are handicapped by their home situation, an obstacle to many a wife and mother to taking on more demanding work, when the comfort of the family is at risk.

Approximately 30% of the women employed in energy production in the German Democratic Republic gave domestic responsibilities as their reason for not wishing to undertake further training. It must be said at the same time that thousands of women can function in their new role at work because their families observe a new and more just division of work. Husbands, above all, save their wives from excessive domestic claims upon their time so that they too can find satisfaction in their chosen work. It is an essential maxim of socialism that nobody has the right to personal comfort at the cost of hindering others in their self-expression.

There are, of course, other and individual reasons which keep many women from developing, and attaining leading positions in their work even with adequate training. There are, as we have mentioned before, the remnants of outmoded thinking concerning woman's role. The argument that men are better in leading positions still holds good in many areas. With those men in superior positions the old ideas die hard and more or less suppressed prejudices persist against the promotion of women. Nowadays these are seldom founded on opposition in principle to women pursuing a career, nor are they first and foremost objections against woman's suitability to hold a leading position in planning or production. More frequent than yesterday's ideological objections, there are other, newer ones which have arisen with the growth of women's equality.

They consist mainly of financial and organizational considerations of some managers concerning the greater vulnerability of women colleagues. These negative considerations

are based mainly on woman's function as mother and her domestic responsibilities. She takes maternity leave, then often remains at home for a while with her child. She has days off for work at home, a shorter but fully paid working week if she has several children and usually takes time off to look after her children when they are sick. Might it therefore not be more logical, the argument goes, to employ only men in leading positions? It is certainly easier and often more "effective", if one does not look beyond the interests of the individual firm, and also if one chooses to forget that all children will grow up and that every woman will then repay, and with interest, the consideration given her by her firm. Any thought which takes in the whole of society makes it completely clear that mere "effectiveness" of the moment cannot be the main concern. It is contrary to the realization of full equality and the stated aims of the socialist order.

Therefore, and this is woman's good fortune, every firm has the duty of building up women to take leading positions, and of overcoming along the way those difficulties arising from women's particular problems. In the planning of posts for women at managerial level, the principle of equal rights, not privileges, is all-important. Favorable conditions for women do not mean, as some maintain, half jokingly perhaps, "the beginning of a new matriarchy", and inflicting wrongs on men. These very conditions exist to help overcome the educational handicaps of many women and the problems arising from their dual function.

On no account does the obtaining of leading positions by women mean their getting into these places at any price. Such beliefs can only damage the cause of equality, and in the individual case lead to failure. Obviously women cannot be put into higher positions without having the required qualifications, simply on the grounds that they are women. A leading position must at all times only be held by a person fully qualified for it. So the main point is to equip as many women as possible with suitable qualifications.

To summarize: the position of women in the socialist economy cannot be compared with the life of working women in the past, not even with the position of women today living under a different social order. There are still problems and difficulties to be overcome, so that all working women may make full use of their equality in the life of the nation and demonstrate clearly the transformed and liberated position of woman in society.

Bencho Obreshkov. Harvest celebration. 1966

Women and Politics

The role woman plays in a socialist democracy is closely linked to her position in the production process of society. Thus woman's path to working equality in a socialist society was at the same time a road to increasing her political activity and democratic participation in decision-making. Democracy means the opportunity for all working people to take a direct part in decisions concerning matters of state and society. How far can women make use of this opportunity offered to them on the same terms as men?

Many prejudices against women taking an active part in political life have practically disappeared under socialism. Women have proved themselves for a long time, and this, along with ideological work in the new society, has gradually undermined existing preconceived notions. It has become rare in a socialist society to have anybody mention the outmoded idea that women should remain silent in the community, or that politics are a matter for men. Such views are laughed at now wherever socialist democracy has become reality, and women take their part actively, naturally and not less successfully than men.

The role of woman in the life of society, the degree of her political emancipation cannot be judged by the public achievement of a few selected women. A female head of state, for example, is as the past and present show, not an expression of the general equality of women in a particular country. Genuine political equality of the women of a country can be measured only by the quantity and quality of their democratic participation in all spheres of public life.

Democracy and participation of women in political decision-making begin in the socialist countries at the lowest level, at the place of work and in the home. Women's steadily growing skills make them more and more capable of participating creatively in production conferences of their factories and in important discussions about economic planning and its realization. Women can make suggestions for rationalization and the improvement of living

FRIENDSHIP

*When you have understood
quite clearly the highest science
—combat—then you will also know
how wonderful and mighty is
the strength of friendship...*

Aleksander Tvardovsky

and working conditions, and thus can take a leading part in innovations in industry and agriculture.

In the industrial councils of Poland—democratic committees of state-owned industry—which exert influence on planning and management, more than a third of the members are women. Nearly 40,000 women in the German Democratic Republic are busy in similar institutions—the permanent advisory committees to industry, forming 22.5% of the entire membership. There are 104,311 women working on the women's committees of factories. These committees also exist in other socialist countries, and represent all the women in a firm. They are elected by them and consist of particularly capable and trustworthy col-

leagues. They make it their duty to act as an extension of the law where women's interests are concerned, trying to secure for them the best possible conditions of life and work. The committees play a positive part in developing the desire for better training, and together with the trade unions further the proper placement of women in responsible positions.

Research done in the Soviet Union has yielded interesting results, showing that women from about 35 to 39 years of age are especially active in industrial production. Sociologists trace this to the fact that the largest number of skilled women workers is concentrated in this age group in the Soviet Union. In other socialist countries too, the proportion of women prepared to be active in society is directly re-

VALENTINA

*When pot and table and bed were invented,
and fires glowed on the cottage hearth,
all was there for domestic bliss.
Then we bound her with her own hair,
bound her to property
and the hearth, her own creation.*

*We owned the world from end to end.
All that made us brave and hungry;
everything that grew, was invented
and had thought was our work,
and owed its existence to man.
And what we saw in our women,
was nothing but ourselves.
To us all spirit was male.*

*But now the hearth's narrow circle has
burst open, like a thistle bloom, firm and ripe,
and a poor hackneyed, stupid lie has died.*

Heinz Kahlau

lated to their level of skilled training. This is particularly so for participation in solving planning and management problems.

Soviet sociologists have rightly pointed out that women are developing a great objective interest in industry. From this there appears to follow that despite the rise in living standards married women will not leave industry; rather, their motivation for work will change. Financial considerations will play a smaller part, and the new motivation develops not least through woman's democratic participation in industry.

In the socialist countries practically all working women belong to a union. For example, half of all trade union members in the Soviet Union, and 41.9% in Bulgaria, are women. In the German Democratic Republic 96 of 100 working women are union members, that is, 48.8% of the total membership. In contrast, the corresponding figure in the German Federal Republic is only 13%.

And the women are not just the "foot soldiers" of the unions. A large number of functionaries on all levels of union work are women. In Bulgaria 46.3% of the women were elected to higher offices in the trade unions. In the German Democratic Republic every third woman union member holds a function, and in 1972 44.6% of all union functionaries were women. In the factory arbitration committees, which hold high authority, there are 23,120 women.

One of the reasons for the activity of working women in public life, particularly young women, is that youth organizations prepare them for this work. Activity in public life, thus realizing one small part of democracy, is taught early to the Young Pioneers, and education for taking part in democratic responsibilities is continued in the youth organizations. In the Soviet Union fourteen million girls and young women are members of the Communist Youth Organization, 50% of the whole membership.

It is not surprising therefore that the female membership of the leading parties in socialist countries is growing. An application to become a member of the working-class party is for many the logical outcome of their knowledge and experience gained in learning and working. Today more than a quarter of all members of the socialist party in the German Democratic Republic are women; 22.9% in Hungary; and 20.5% in Poland.

A number of women find their way to political activity via all kinds of community work, work which is initiated by the socialist movement, including all parties and organizations. In this movement in the residential areas of towns and villages, women's organizations play a large and progressive part. They see it as their task constantly to develop women's political self-confidence, and to guide them towards their public duties. In the Patriotic People's Front in Hungary, 1,800 women's committees were formed with a large membership. In the committees of the National Front in the German Democratic Republic, 103,000 women are at work, 30% of the membership. In the Fatherland Front of Bulgaria, 83,609 of 203,700 leading members are women.

Thus for many women participation in public life begins at their own front door, in the social committees which bring people more closely together, organize neighborly help,

Preceding double page:

*They have come
from all over the world,
And their subject is:* PEACE.

Walter Womacka. Women hoeing turnips. 1956

The village has completely changed, with a fine large house of culture, a swimming pool, a new school, a nursery and crèche. It has asphalted roads and a system of drainage.

The people also have changed, in particular the women. They have set hours of work and more leisure than ever before; they have gone to school again and are now skilled workers, used to working with modern mechanical equipment. Most of them treat themselves to a holiday away every year.

Whenever before did a village woman have a holiday, and a paid one at that?

Maria's son is now working on his diploma thesis on pig-breeding. A daughter was born to the couple after him, and she, too, is grown up and has begun studying to become an agricultural engineer.

If Maria is asked what she considers the best thing socialism has brought to the countryside, she replies without hesitation: "The best thing is cooperation and the new relationship of people, one to the other. The best is the friendship in the village."

There are even richer and more modern collectives than the one Maria and her family work in. There is, for example, Trinvillershagen in formerly poor Mecklenburg. The barns and stables of this village are now like factory halls, and the people—men and women alike —are highly skilled. There are more than 20 college-trained farmers, 46 holding diplomas, 294 skilled workers, 181 experts, drivers of cranes and tractors, mechanics, etc. Medical institutions are excellent, and the sports stadium and bowling alley should be ready by now. Twenty-eight women work huge combines, and these women cannot be compared

to their mothers and grandmothers who humbled themselves when they passed the landowner's mansion.

Many similar tales could be told of the agricultural collectives in other countries. There is the Bulgarian collective of Dalgopol, combining nine villages and working 12,000 hectares—some 30,000 acres. Women in this collective are highly specialized and modern, with expectations in life quite unthinkable for their mothers and grandmothers. The agricultural collectives in the Soviet Union, in Bulgaria, Rumania, Hungary, Czechoslovakia and the German Democratic Republic differ widely in size, wealth of machinery, crops, income and cultural level. But they all have one thing in common: they bring people together, help to overcome the difference between town and country and allow the village woman to free herself from the curse of discrimination and feeling of inferiority. The biggest part in this process of liberation has again been played by the women themselves. If one were to ask the chairman of a collective in Hungary or Rumania or any other socialist country for a list of the most faithful and best members, he or she would certainly give such names as Tina, Natasha, Ruzena, Lilya, Sanda, Halina, Margarete and Maria.

A visit to a remote Siberian collective remains unforgettable. It was near Lake Baikal, not far from Irkutsk, and not more wonderful than many others. Here lives Katyusha Sarotkina, an animal husbandry expert who works in the highly mechanized dairy of the collective. Our visit was unexpected, and the young woman's face glowed as in a flash she brought to the table whatever good things she could

find in the house: preserves, cake, pickles, tea and vodka. No earthly power can stop a Russian peasant woman from entertaining her guests. At last she sat down, and, raising her glass, greeted us with the beautiful dignity native to Russian women. Her husband, the veterinary surgeon of the collective, and her three children came into the room, also the children's grandparents, Pavel Nikolaevich and Stepanida Ivanovna. They were born in the village, and remembered it with its brutal poverty, its dirt and its ignorance.

The old peasant said: "When we founded our collective we did not dream of such a good life. Nobody could even imagine it. Only perhaps Lenin." But then Katyusha talked about the present. She talked about the culture of the village, the highly profitable cultivation of early vegetables, the free clinic with a modern department of obstetrics, the nursery and the crèche. She also spoke of twenty-five young people studying at universities with grants supplied by the collective. She talked about herself being the chairwoman of the parents' advisory committee at the school, and how she loved animals, above all the 250 cows, 70 young cattle and 200 calves under her care.

Then old Stepanida Ivanovna suggested to Katyusha: "Tell our guests about Cuba." Katyusha and her husband had been in Cuba for a holiday, and these two people from eastern Siberia also knew Algiers. "Many people from our village go on such journeys. The collective pays 70% of the costs." The young woman spoke with enthusiasm. "The friendship of the people is tremendous everywhere in the world. When they heard that we

Iván Szabo. Girls picking flowers

When the sun scatters
his gold on the corn,
the wind anticipates
the scent of fresh bread,
carrying it into towns and villages.
If only the wind was always right.

Eva Haase

The Changed Face of the Countrywoman

Perhaps the most obvious and striking change has come about in the life of those women who in the past were the most backward and the poorest, namely the women in the villages.

They have moved on a path which was difficult at first, the path of becoming collective farmers. We will follow this path through the example of a particular woman, to show how her life has changed.

When the estates of landed proprietors were parcelled out after the war, our peasant woman—let us call her Maria G.—received a plot of land. Like all the other peasants she walked again and again around her holding from one end to the other; and like the others, she again and again took up a handful of soil to see how good it was. She thought it fair and proper that those who had for ages worked the soil should now own it.

Her husband returned from being a prisoner of war and told her that he had become a communist. They built themselves a house of home-made bricks and they had one cow. Life chances in the villages were still very poor, and it meant everyone for himself as it had always been. When the couple's first son was born, and the cow was not in milk, Maria G. did not find the neighbors ready to help. "You shouldn't have children in times like these, and then you wouldn't need milk," they said. Kindness does grow very slowly.

Maria and her husband worked hard, and eventually, like most others in the village, got on. As soon as they had two horses, four cows and two heifers in the barn they could relax, and they were pleased with what they had achieved.

Then in the early 60's "comrades" arrived from the town to tell them clearly what had been in the air for some time. Socialist ways of production, they said, should now be introduced in the countryside too. Further development of agriculture was possible only through collective production on a large scale, which meant agricultural collectives. This was a difficult step to take, as love for one's very own little property is deep-seated. But after a few days and nights of thinking things over, Maria G. said to her husband: "Sign. Times have changed, and socialists have to make the first move." At that time, too, she went to the party secretary of the village, asking to be enrolled. "I have now reached the stage," she told him.

With her husband she worked in the cattle yard, and both gave all their strength to the task in hand. Maria was highly regarded in the village, and besides working in the collective, she was very interested in matters concerning the women. She won over many to joining the women's organization, and she herself trained to become a skilled worker, and a few years later obtained a certificate in pig-breeding.

After its early teething troubles the collective became wealthy, and, after first joining with four and then with nine other collectives with the aim of industrial production, it is now prospering.

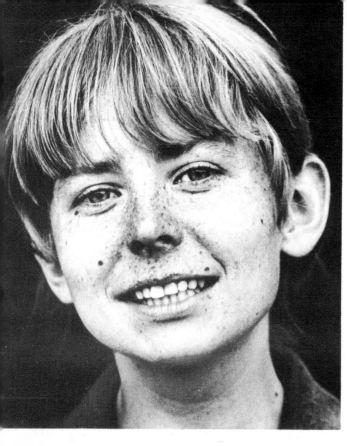

TO ALL
WHOSE
PASSPORT
CARRIES
THE REMARK:
FEMALE

*Even though we may tell ourselves
a hundred times that you—skin,
muscle and nerve—
are nothing but an assembly
of cells, cellular nuclei,
cellulose and protoplasm.*

Calculable, workable
  like steel and concrete—
  Eiffel Tower, Dam of Bratsk,
  cooking pots and washing poles.
But in the breath of your skin,
  with a step or a look
  our logic explodes.

You conform to no formula.
You dare us into combat
  with ourselves.
Each word—exam, each step—
  start into space.
You are the unadulterated scale
  that we preserve.

Who with you fails, fails with himself.
And who succeeds,
  may well be trusted to tackle
  the next stage of building
  at the Angara dams.

Joochen Laabs

create playgrounds and sports facilities, meet for discussions, and much else. Women's initiative is important in the parents' committees of crèches and nurseries, in the advisory committees of socialist industry and trade, and, above all, in schools. In nearly all socialist countries half of the parents' committees in schools are women, sometimes even up to two thirds.

Especially responsible community work is done by members of the arbitration committees to whom the police hand over, for example, the hearing of certain misdemeanors of local residents. These committees also arbitrate disputes which disturb the home, and help juveniles in trouble back to the right road. Very many women work in these committees, making up 37.1% of all elected members in the German Democratic Republic. Community political work is democracy and equality in action. For many women this is the step preparing them for their work as a delegate representing the people at large.

Women's participation is most advanced in the people's political representation of the Soviet Union. Women represent 46% of all delegates of workers to the Soviets, nearly one million from all the nationalities of the Soviet Union. Half of the delegates in the Moscow City Soviet are women, and the highest body of the state, the Supreme Soviet, counts 463 women among its members, that is, 31% of all delegates. Yadgar Nasriddinova from Uzbekistan holds the high position of chairman of the Soviet of Nationalities, one of the two chambers of the Supreme Soviet. In the governments of the Union Republics there are 28 women ministers.

The majority of the delegates are women workers and peasants. One of them, the young delegate Syssoeva, spoke with gaiety of a journey by a youth delegation to the United States. The delegation was able to gather many impressions of country and people. A meeting was organized with Senators to show the young people how American democracy works. "I was asked who I was, and I answered: 'Delegate to the Supreme Soviet of the Russian Federal Republic, my normal work is as a dairy-maid'."

In the Soviet Union 32.3% of the elected people's judges and 48% of the magistrates are women. In the German Democratic Republic 45% of the magistrates are women.

In the other socialist countries, too, women workers and peasants in high public office are no longer rare. In Bulgaria the number of women delegates has more than doubled since 1949, and in Rumania 31% of all delegates are women, with about the same percentage in the German Democratic Republic.

How much the life of woman in socialist society has changed becomes particularly clear when her position in politics is compared to that of women in the Western countries:

Proportion of Women in Parliament (in 1972)

Finland	21.5%
Denmark	16.8%
Sweden	14.0%
Norway	10.0%
German Federal Republic	5.8%
Great Britain	4.1%
USA	2.8%
Canada	0.3%

Even looking at these statistics illustrating women's progress under socialism, it must be stressed that there is no smugness in the socialist countries. The proportion of women in the total number of delegates, and their influence in politics, must increase still further if they are to correspond to real equality of the sexes and the part woman is to play in the economy and in public life as a whole. The tendency certainly is clearly in the direction of equality. As the prejudices mentioned before vanish there also vanishes the old idea of "politics spoiling character". This can surely only hold good for politics directed from above, and directed against the interests of the people. When, however, politics come from "below", when masses of people, among them great numbers of women, work together for the common good, rise above the immediate interests and wishes of the individual and act accordingly, politics can only develop character. Being active in the community willl strengthen woman's self-confidence and alow her to overcome the frustrations and narrowness of exclusively domestic life. It will develop her public spirit, making her into a genuine partner in the struggle for the solution of major social problems. It will extend her maternal qualities beyond the limits of her own family, enabling her to feel one with all the oppressed people of the world. The massive political activity of women under socialism is one of the most gratifying results of revolutionary transformation, and a precondition for the overcoming of contradictions and problems which still handicap a great number of women in making use of their equality in all spheres of life.

The hen wife is not a fairy.
Her feet are planted
firmly on the ground,
and her hands do not work magic.
She looks to the future,
and shapes her life
accordingly with work,
thought, dancing and love,
and learning again and again.
A "life with hens"?
Yes, a life with hens, and one
with a great future.

Cocks still
fight eachother,
dogs bite eachother
for bones,
and sows eat
their young.

But men
have become human.

Helmut Preissler

Yuri Milovich Tulin.
T. Kislyakova, the best agricultural engineer
of the state-owned estate "Melnikov". 1961

Viktor Pavlovich Kabanov. Pioneering life. 1961

were peasants from a Siberian collective, many embraced us or simply touched us." We asked Katyusha how it felt to return from such adventures to the village collective. "Excellent," she said, "fine, that's perhaps the best thing of the whole journey."

We have also personal experience of the life of women in the Petöfi collective in Lipót, or the Hungarian agricultural combine of Bélásizza, consisting of about 40,000 acres, and cultivating mainly fruit and tobacco. We might mention a Rumanian peasant woman who is in charge of a state-owned estate, and of the special worries of a chairman of an Ukrainian collective who is urgently looking for a ballet teacher and a football trainer for the young people of her village. There is much more to tell, but let a few interesting facts suffice: in the Czechoslovakian countryside five times more young women are educated than their fathers and eight times more than their mothers. In Bulgaria 58% of the trained farmers are women, and 36% of the agronomists. In the German Democratic Republic in recent years more women working in agriculture have received specialized certificates than men. Also, their exam results were better. While in 1966 only 19.6% of the women in an agricultural collective successfully completed specialized training, the proportion rose to 40% in 1971. And the numbers have risen further in the meantime.

There are naturally still many problems and contradictions for women in socialist agriculture, and when some are solved, new ones do turn up. But these problems—as with women workers and professional women—are no longer women's problems but the prob-

lems of a whole society. At the moment it is necessary through further mechanization to ease women's labor in the fields, and to orientate some countrywomen, within the framework of intensive mechanization, towards entirely new activities. The number of women working in managerial positions in agriculture must also be increased.

What made Katyusha Sarotkina happy on returning to her Siberian village, battling against winter for many months of the year, not minding leaving exotic warm lands behind, is not just the joy of seeing her children again, or a sentimental feeling for home. More than anything it is the bond which ties her to the people of the village. She has missed them, and they are waiting for her. And Maria G., the peasant woman from the German Democratic Republic, believes, as we have seen, that friendship and the human relationships are the best of all the things socialism has brought. The acceptance of this new community feeling, the joy in it, and the value to the individual is not limited to life in the villages, though in the country the results are perhaps most obvious and foreseeable. The rural community has always been more closely knit, yet the new and friendly relationships also mark life in the cities.

How does this new sense of belonging come about? Not, of course, through ideological campaigns. The socialist community—in smaller or bigger units—has its main roots in the new concepts of property. Had, for example, Maria G. remained an individual peasant on her own small piece of land, all her thought and effort, her ideas and activities, would have been directed first and foremost towards

what was hers. Nobody could have expected her to say: "The best of all good things is the community."

The socialist concept of property unites people in the work process, working for wealth to be achieved by all. The individual recognizes that his personal interest is inextricably bound up with that of the community. He recognizes that in the long run nothing can be of use to him which is harmful to the community in which he lives and works. This is the basis from which develops in a complicated and often contradictory process, full of positive and negative experiences, tensions and arguments, and influenced by bigger and smaller successes, that kind of behavior indigenous to socialist ideology. It is a solidarity among people, a sincere interest in the advancement of others, readiness to help, and a feeling of responsibility for the common good.

A small but typical example may illustrate this particular characteristic of human relationships. In a factory in Prague, 26 women formed a working group. One of them, Vera Schwarzova, died, leaving behind a son. The whole group of women became godmothers to the boy, who was cared for by his grandmother. They looked after him, not just getting him clothes, but helping him at the same time to grow up into a decent person. In the diary of the group there are preserved letters and cards which Peter sent from Pioneer camps. The boy was to find that whatever his difficulties, worries or needs, there were people feeling close to him. When he became an apprentice, training to be a car mechanic, somewhere in Bohemia, his mother's work group fitted him out in a way his own mother

154

could not have improved on. They also sent a letter to Peter's future supervisor, asking him to give Peter his special attention. "Let us know," they said, "how he is getting on. We shall help." Regularly these women put money into the savings bank for "their son". "When he comes out of the army we shall give him the accumulated money so that he will have a good start." And as for Peter: "I am glad that I have them. I know the world cannot be altogether bad."

These basically harmonious personal relationships in the community and in working collectives do not mean that there are no conflicts. On the contrary. The ferment of any socialist community are the impatient people, in conflict always between good and better, dragging the whole collective into their own conflict which, hardly solved, raises its head again, and keeps things on the move.

There is a poem from present-day Bulgaria, in praise of "fighting". It was written by Pavel Matev, and reads:

We fight
About words
About Books
About Steel
About ourselves
About
what is there in abundance
About
what is still missing.
Nobody
gives us the right
not to fight.
Too much remains undone.
Remembering this, we fight till we are hoarse.

Let nobody think
that fighting divides us.
If we had to fight again in earnest
tomorrow
then, more than ever,
would we be united.

An example for a fighting yet beneficial force in the community is the woman worker Christel Krüger. Forty years old, and for twenty of these, half of her life, she worked at the Carl-von-Ossietzky works in Teltow in the German Democratic Republic. She grew up during the war, the eldest of four children in a worker's family. After her schooling she worked on the land, then a few years in a household, with no grand plans. But at fourteen she became a member of a union. "So that you can get justice," her father told her. When she met the man who was to become her husband, he persuaded her to leave domestic work and go into a factory. "To make your work worthwhile," he said. It was soon discovered that Christel had "golden hands", and not only were her hands considered, but her whole person. She was possessed of complete honesty and reliability, and her natural readiness to do her best showed the way she had been brought up, conscious and proud of her class. And they said: "She will become one of us. She is of the stuff socialists are made of."

She joined the working group *Völkerfreundschaft* (Friendship among Peoples), and of this first collective the very rational Christel Krüger now talks in an almost tender way. It is here that she gathered her perhaps most important experience, namely that work in a collective not only multiplies people's achievement but

gives it potential. In a community where one works and argues, fights and agrees with like-minded people, and fights again, always looking ahead, in such a community the impossible becomes possible, and mountains can be moved. It was this experience above all which in the course of ten years made a determined socialist of the young worker. It made a busily turning cog into a self-propelled motor.

Later Christel became a member of another working collective, carrying the name of a brave resistance fighter against fascism, "Olga Benario". Everybody in the factory speaks with respect of the "Benarios", and with great pride of "our Olgas". There used to be an idea that a working group consisting of women only was a contradiction, as by nature, it was said, women were individualists, and, because of their competition for a man, were, again by nature, enemies of one another. However, the contrary of this assumption is proved day after day by millions in the socialist countries. The "Benarios" became a genuine community.

Is it then all work and duty, as certain writers state, when they describe woman's life under socialism? Surely, none of the "Benarios" would have been happy with that sort of existence. Life in a socialist society should be fun too. It also means that the individual should not be swamped by society, but rather that society should help the individual to develop his or her personality to the full. This concept of the relation of the individual to society is as old as scientific socialism.

Marx and Engels believed that only being in a community with others would supply the individual with the means of fully developing his or her capacities, and that only within this

Wolfgang Wegener.
Bookkeeper in an agricultural collective and his wife. 1972

community would personal freedom be fully achieved. (32)

Christel Krüger, grown into a personality within the community, loves her evening leisure as much as all her colleagues do. She loves her weekends with her husband and children, is pleased with the small house she lives in, and tells of her many helpful relatives. But soon she talks again about her "Olgas". Pointing to the open terrace in front of her house, she relates: "Here we had a grand birthday celebration, and then we went off together on our shift. It was a good experience."

Out of the community life of most working people and out of the socialist attitude to property, gained over the years, comes a phenomenon remarked on by a Swedish journalist visiting Hungary. He conveyed his impression vividly when he said: "Every tenth word they speak is 'we' and every eleventh 'our'."

Generally the young generation has a positive attitude towards the collective. They do not have to make the difficult transfer from the "I" to the "we" that their parents and grandparents had to make.

According to a tradition of the socialist workers' movement young people—at the age of fourteen—celebrate in the GDR the day when they become members of the adult community. And here is a quotation from a speech made to mark that day: "Use your head, use your hands, and your heart. But take care of your elbows. You do not need them to get on in life as your parents did."

This is perhaps the best that socialism has achieved—that we can say with conviction: save your elbows, and use them only to "feel" the people next to you.

Precious Leisure

Leisure is precious not only because it is still scarce in the life of a working woman but equally because it supplies relaxation and renews energy. Life under socialism is meant to have quality, and provide joy in people's everyday life, joy in work and in play. There should not be a sharp division, that alienation which Marx has described as: "The working man feeling at home only when work is finished, and feeling alienated at work." (33)

Gradually the contrast between working hours and leisure is vanishing as people get closer to enjoying life unfragmented. Sometimes women's existence under socialism is presented as consisting of work and study only. However, there is much else, and in a socialist society woman has all the means to enjoy her leisure to the full. Houses of culture, vacation homes and sports facilities serve to provide a wide variety of leisure activities.

Added to these are the many new interests taken up by men and women, even more noticeably by women whose world, not very long ago, was so much narrower than man's. Training and careers have changed all that, and research in the Soviet Union has obtained the following interesting results (34):

In Leningrad 1,488 women workers were asked about their favorite subjects of conversation among friends and relatives. It was shown that the subjects were more demanding with skilled workers than among women with elementary education only. Subjects for women workers with intermediate, technical and higher education ranked as follows:

a) problems of work and career
b) art
c) politics
d) mutual friends
e) domestic questions of the day

Women workers with elementary education provided the following results:

a) domestic questions of the day
b) art
c) career problems
d) mutual friends
e) politics

It is significant that all groups set great store by art, and indeed art plays an important part in the life of almost every woman (and, of course, man) in the Soviet Union, a fact foreign visitors often remark on, with some astonishment. One must experience the audience reaction in a Russian theater to understand the enthusiasm and the critical ability. One can sense the temperamental and emotional involvement with what is going on on the stage whether it concerns a play, a concert, a ballet or folk entertainment. And the public consists of people from all strata of society, with many workers and peasants.

These close relationships of large numbers of people with art are an immediate result of the cultural revolution which made reality of the slogan: "Art for the People". The same trend can be noticed in other countries building a socialist society. Hundreds of thousands took their first step into a theater, a concert hall or an art gallery just because the others did it, yet half doubting whether it was a step for simple folk to take.

Many collectives have literally fought for their first understanding of works of art, often assisted by actors, musicians, painters and people connected with the world of film-making.

The writer Marta Nawrath has described a woman worker's visit to a concert in a poem:

A Worker in the Coal Mine Visits a Concert

The party says: the working class
must conquer the heights of culture.
Working class, I'm part of it
So I went and bought
a ticket for the concert.

To begin with I played with the clasp
of my little glittering handbag.
It was new—everything was new—
also that I sat in a concert,
I, a worker in the coal mine.

Does the woman next to me
know what that means? She reads the score
as others read their newspapers.
Does she know how exact my work has to be
for the coal to roll along smoothly?

The programme says
   "Allegro" and "Andante".
I know not what it means.
But I will know tomorrow.
Will she know tomorrow
what my work means in the mine?

It does not matter. It matters more that
   I shall learn
what "Allegro" means. No, that's not
   important either.
Important alone is that the music
took me onto the ocean, into a tempest
and to a quiet garden.

I did not go by streetcar,
nor did I take a taxi—
though now and again I can afford to;
I walked all the way
with music around me.

My heart beats strongly and quickly,
just as if I had climbed a mountain.
A mountain with a wonderful view.

Two things are striking in this simple poem: the telling way it describes the working woman's joy, and ability to listen to music, and the strong involvement of the writer with the way art is absorbed by those who in the past had to make do with the second best. Together with the interest of the working class in art goes a changed relationship between artists and public. There exists a completely new kind of popularity for a man or woman artist which has nothing at all to do with commercial publicity. A little incident, observed at a state reception for notable women on International Women's Day, may illustrate this new relationship:

A peasant from a collective farm who had just received a decoration noticed a famous actress and went up to her on the spur of the moment. "We know each other," she said. Actually the two women had met for the first time, but the peasant woman had seen the actress play a peasant woman's part in a television film, and this made her think: this woman knows me well, my life, my joys and my sorrows. And I know her. In many ways she must be similar to me, things close to her heart are surely close to mine. And the actress understood the peasant at once, and agreed happily: "Of course, we know each other."

The worker's theater
of her factory is rehearsing.
Maybe, the young woman
has just left her work
for a glimpse
of what is happening;
to see how the new play
is getting on.
Maybe, she is one
of the actors,
waiting for her cue . . .
Then she belongs
to the many thousands
whose lives
have been enriched by art,
by creativeness, providing
a source of new joys
for themselves and others.
She knows the pains taken
to comprehend a work of art,
the discipline required and
the responsibility of working
in a team with others.
She will become
more versatile, more able,
and her work will confirm
Albert Einstein's opinion
that art accelerates thought . . .

That easy identifying with the audience is perhaps the most satisfying thing for the socialist artist because it makes him aware of his newly found popularity.

Socialism demands a great deal from its artists. They are not expected merely to be experts in their subject; their very popularity makes thousands feel: You are one of us, you give all you possess. You are absolutely honest, and we trust you.

Good artists are much loved in the socialist countries. The closer the relation of the masses becomes to art, the greater their ability to discriminate, the deeper becomes their affection for those who bring art to them, and that in a masterly manner. But there is no star cult. Not that there is a law against it, but it simply has no chance to develop. No serious artist has the wish to become a star because the mere idea conjures up the publicity stunt by which stars are made. And there is no sensational press to advance a star cult by acquainting the public with such important facts as the vital statistics, the latest affairs, the favorite color or car of the divine actor or actress. Working people not only take an interest in art, they are also active in many areas. There are no statistics available yet about the many groups of people painting, writing, making films or music and singing. These exist in great numbers, and many of them are women.

In Lithuania and Estonia alone there are thousands of women singing in the traditional choirs. Amateur actresses, women painters and musicians abound.

One of our illustrations shows an almost empty theater hall. A young woman sits in the first row. Perhaps she has only left work for a short glimpse, maybe she is one of the actresses. Anyhow, she has forgotten to take off her protective helmet. Fascinated she follows the happenings on stage. It is a rehearsal of her firm's drama group, one of the many manifestations of the cultural revolution.

Practically all these groups in industry and agriculture are responsible for creating new mutual relationships between artists and working people. And both parties profit from this give and take, which is an established relationship in the Soviet Union, become tradition by now. The actors of the Mossoviet Theater in Moscow adopted the drama group of a large firm of roller-bearing makers in the 1930's. The group began under primitive conditions in a small club room, when the men and women workers had just learned to read and write. These early amateur actors have now given way at the work benches to a younger generation with higher education, equal and critical partners of the actors, most of them a younger generation also. The actors work regularly with this amateur group, which has attained great quality and dares tackling difficult productions. The firm's house of culture is packed when they are playing.

And why do women workers, peasants, employees of all sorts, doctors and engineers, act in plays, make music or paint? Certainly not to train for a new career; rather, they want a fuller life, developing the artistic abilities which everybody possesses to a greater or lesser degree. The extent to which a person makes use of these gifts is important to him for his full realization and development. Developing these artistic abilities together with others makes for discipline, a sense of community and

Volker Beier. Young girl. 1971

Erhard Grossmann. Painting circle. 1969

WOMAN ARTIST
BEFORE A SCULPTURE

Something is taking shape, perhaps
only something small, yet it is
part of a creator's joy,
a piece of communication,
a piece of personal progress,
in seeking and finding.

GISELA MAY

Wherever in the world
her voice is heard,
People listen enraptured.
What makes her greatness?
It is her richness of talent,
her strange versatility,
the strength of her emotions,
the charm of her personality.

But there are other
sources to her art,
equally important
for the "phenomenon Gisela May".
She travels to New York
but also to little towns
in the Ore Mountains,
to give pleasure to the people there,
and to hear from them

what their lives are like,
and what they think.
Rather than parties
she visits big works,
is with "her brigade" to whom
she gives and from whom she takes.
She is a socialist, believing
that her art will help to change
the world and people.

the ability to fit individually into a greater whole—virtues useful in all spheres of life.

With women, artistic pursuits contribute to self-confidence, and for them singing, dancing, acting or painting opens new windows on life, in addition to providing a source of pleasure for themselves and others. If women were told that art was necessary to life to enable everybody to understand the world, and to change it, many might shake their heads and smile. Could music really change the world? All the same, precisely that is possible. This is, of course, not an immediate result. The world is not changed by waves of sound, but in a roundabout way music does influence the development of the individual. Art makes each person aware of himself, clearer about his thoughts and his emotions. He learns to think more profoundly and feel more deeply. Man is also in need of art because of its simple enchantment. And does woman in socialist society need this very enchantment? Not an enchantment to escape from the realities of this world, but the enchantment that enriches and broadens all life.

Socialist education, both in theory and practice, is fully aware of these forces, and begins in the nursery to lead children towards creative activities and enjoyment of the arts, possible at that stage of the child's development. An example of the early discovery and nurturing of talent is the story of the young highly gifted dancer Nadezhda Pavlova, which we have related beside her photograph.

Just as talent in the arts is discovered and guided early, so is a gift for any kind of sport, thus providing over and over again new and active generations of youth. Nearly all well-known women athletes have emerged from children's sports training. For many women sports fill much of their leisure time. Groups of gymnasts, all under expert guidance, are increasingly popular in industry and in community areas.

Reading, too, forms part of women's leisure. It has been shown that women in socialist countries read much more than their counterparts living under different systems. This is most obvious in the Soviet Union. A writer from the German Federal Republic, on a visit to the Soviet Union, remarked that he found a whole nation reading. "They read," he said, "while out shopping, on the motor boat on the Dnepr, in the gondola of the mountain railway in the Carpathians, and in the collectives of the Western Ukraine. Natasha even reads on the escalators of the Moscow subway."

This writer was interested, too, in the question of what was being read, and whether some sort of "fixed" subjects were the favorites. "I notice," he wrote, "that the eternal subjects of literature are preferred here too: love, hate, birth, death and again and again, love, love and love." (35)

A writer from the German Democratic Republic, Christa Wolf, has written a book on reading and writing, and poses the question: what would it mean if suddenly all traces of the influence of books vanished? This, she concludes, would be a very bad thing, because, "How could I guess that the world around me is full of wonder, peopled often by the strangest figures, that it is full of adventure, some just waiting for me to take part in them. In short, I would not have gone back to the beginning of things, not have drunk at the source, and I would have nothing to measure people and things by. Nothing could ever make up for the loss. A world that at the right time was not mysterious and enchanted, does not become clearer with growing knowledge, but arid." And Christa Wolf finishes with the thought: "I myself, without books, would not be myself."

Other peoples, too, who with the coming of socialism have overcome illiteracy, have meanwhile become great readers. Rumyana Gautsheva, a Bulgarian writer, has reported about the beginning of reading in the village of Boshurishte. She tells of a village drama group buying books with their first earnings. "It was the spark which lit inextinguishable fires. A library. But only a few read books; they did not feel like it. Freedom was born, but there was still so much to be done." Rumyana Gautsheva tells how the secretary from the house of culture went from door to door with books. And she persuaded a peasant woman to take a book. But only the next day her child returned it unread. The librarian went back to the house for a second time: "Look," she said, "I am sure you had no time to read the book, and it's very good. So I'll tell you the story just while you are working."

And a beginning was made.

When nowadays at village feasts such tales are told in Bulgaria, Rumania, Yugoslavia, Hungary or Poland, often with names and addresses, everybody laughs and is greatly amused. Only very few people in the socialist countries do not count reading as part of their lives.

To women, of course, leisure does not just mean artistic activities, hobbies or reading.

Vera Nedkova. Self-portrait. 1970

A new star has risen
in the world of ballet,
Nadezhda Pavlova.
Seventeen years only,
and already
one of the great
whose grace and mastery
amazes the experts.
She is the child
of a family of workers,
from Perm
in the distant Urals.

Her career began
in "quite an ordinary way",
in the choreography group
of her Pioneer Palace,
one of the tens of thousands of groups
where hundreds and thousands

of Soviet children dance,
to learn body control and gain grace.
Only few of them
want to become dancers.
But Nadya wanted to
at any price.

Her new fame still makes her shy.
But soon her star
will shine on all the world.

A. A. Chuikov. Kirghiz girl with melon. 1956
Friedrun Bondzin. The concert. 1968

Dear horse,
it's truly wrong to say
that your value is lost
through motorized vans.

Dear horse, you needn't cry,
nor feel ashamed.
Good times will come:
when my grandchildren,
in the morning,
before travelling in a rocket,
will ride you for an hour
around the starting pad.

Sarah Kirsch

Bert Heller.
Girls in the shower room. 1964

Miklós Varga. Stepping into the water

At times it means, first and foremost, studying. Many women devote part of their leisure to helping in schools, communities or women's organizations and people's committees. Last not least, no small part of woman's leisure belongs to her family, particularly to the children. It has been calculated that on an average 50% of the leisure of working women is taken up by their children.

We have shown a wide variety of leisure activities but by no means all of them. All possibilities are used increasingly, and have already helped to shape a new type of woman. Yet our picture would not be complete without mentioning at the same time that woman, within the means at her disposal and in her leisure possibilities, is still, by and large, not on an equal footing with man. There is even a danger that many women will again be left behind in cultural developments. The heavy load many working women carry with caring for and raising children, and with housework, severely limits their opportunities for using their leisure in artistic and social activities or sports. In these as in other areas mentioned, all efforts of society are now directed towards creating conditions enabling women to use their equality to the full.

And what are the measures which can be taken to increase the leisure of working mothers? Shorter working hours? Certainly, everything points to a shorter working day for all working people. But until society has the means it requires, there is still much work to be done, and more time will pass. The Soviet sociologist B. Grushin has given an answer to the question, expressing a popular view held by women themselves. He says: "In the struggle to increase leisure the main attack should not be on working hours, but on the hours away from work, that is, on those things which use up energy without developing personality." (36)

The biggest reserve of leisure for woman can be tapped by reducing her household commitments to a minimum. These still take a maximum of strength in exchange for a minimum of effectiveness.

PARACHUTISTS

The sky
won't let me fall
any longer;
Mother Earth
holds me in her vision.
I tidy the ropes,
and take direction
towards the landing signs.
Between
two phases of exercise
I forsake Mother Earth.
But the steely face
above guards me.
All well?
I wave upwards.
Mother Earth, we're coming.

Charlotte Bechstein

Children — Privileged Citizens

Woman remains the mother. Nobody should take from her this, her finest role. The question of whether working women make good mothers has long since ceased to be a question. It was given a clear answer by Clara Zetkin in 1896 when she spoke on equality at the party congress in Gotha. It was then difficult to combine motherhood and a career, but then as now this was the foundation for equality in family life. Clara Zetkin described love, marriage and motherhood as "the indestructible roots of the physical and mental life of every woman." But these are not the only roots, as woman is not just a sexual being. She is a human being, a female human being. "Her wish to be active," said Clara Zetkin, "is not exhausted through fulfillment in the limited sphere of the uniquely feminine. It strongly demands opportunities for growth and expansion beyond."

Growth and expansion—no mother desires these at the expense of her children's happiness. Her own well-being and happiness are bound up with those of her children. Professor Rudolf Neubert, a scholar whose work is popular in the socialist countries, and who has been a life-long medical sociologist and family adviser, answers the question of what a child needs to grow up happily in this way:

"Children need warmth. But I am not happy to see the needs of our children put on the level with those of young birds. The "warmth of the nest" is a concept often misunderstood. The warmth children need is by no means spoiling them or always fussing around them. What children do need is a home to which the family returns gladly after a busy working day. They need father's and mother's loving interest, need them to share their joys and to help them overcome their own little difficulties and worries. There are wonderful parents who on working days can spend but two hours with the children, yet use this time properly. There are less good parents where at least one of them is around the children all day."

It is obvious that working mothers on the whole have wider interests, and are more stimulated by a greater variety of influences. They may themselves be studying, and may therefore be better partners and helpers to their children, particularly to those who are studying themselves, than non-working mothers. One can, of course, not make an absolute statement, as with changed ways of life generalizations are dangerous. These changed ways of life have created work in communities, schools and women's organizations which

R. Kiss Lenke. Girls reading

opens up new fields to those women forced to stay at home, particularly to mothers of several children, only able to work part-time.

A working mother will experience a conflict between her inclination to follow a career outside the home and love of her children, for whom she wants to be assured of good care during her working day. When these problems arise most women decide, as any good mother would, in favor of the children.

For many women the solution to their problems is still the possession of a good grandmother. She will look after the home and the children while the young woman can go out to work carefree, can study and perfect herself. But the number of grandmothers willing and able to look after children decreases every year, even in the Soviet Union, the classic country for caring and always ready *babushkas*. Today's grandmothers stay young longer, and many of them have a career themselves which they cling to and hope to continue in as long as possible. In the 285 new towns of the Soviet Union, naturally towns of young people, a grandmother is now a very rare thing. The real solution of the problem is the establishment of modern institutions for child care. More and more infants are entrusted to crèches in the socialist countries. With excellent conditions prevailing most children thrive, a sound enough argument in the still topical discussion as to whether infants should be left in crèches or not and at what age.

In this discussion some experts in the Soviet Union, for example Professor Urlanis, plead or woman's right to take a year's leave after a birth, with security of tenure at her place of work. Even after that, say the experts, a woman

should, if possible, look after her child for another two years. (37) (Of 4,200,000 children born in the Soviet Union in 1970, only 171,000 were taken care of in crèches.) Other medical sociologists, doctors and educators have different views, holding that in the second year of a child's life, in particular, language and thinking develop, as well as early patterns of behavior. These need not be confined to the family but may extend to a group of children, where "sports" and celebrations, birthdays, for example, will help to form the ability to experience things in a community. It is stressed, however, that for the well-being of an infant a very close contact must exist between parents and crèche, bringing about a harmonious working together of crèche and home. There is bound to be further discussion of the subject but in practice there are still far too few places in crèches.

A much noticed and interesting solution has been found in Hungary. There, in 1967, a system of child subsidy was introduced, consisting essentially of granting working women "child money" for three years after birth, up to 600 forints per month. Women can decide for themselves whether or not to go on working during this period. The system has met with much acclaim by Hungarian women. In 1972 some 8% had temporarily interrupted their work. In some other socialist countries, including the Soviet Union, similar measures may be introduced, though many sociologists maintain that the "Hungarian solution" only temporarily suppresses the conflict between motherhood and career. The fact remains that woman, by interrupting her work for a considerable time, is in danger of stagnating, particularly when there is another child after a short interval. The better trained the woman, the greater the danger. Knowledge now becomes obsolete very quickly, and once the child is three years old, the family is faced again with the same problem, only postponed: career and study on one side, and care for the child and housework on the other.

Gyula Hinczo.
Mother with child and dove. 1959

I HAVE LISTENED TO
THE NEW LIFE

in your body:
suddenly the children love me
and talk to me.

Helmut Preissler

Every second a human being
is born in this world,
a new light is lit,
a star which may sparkle
uncommonly brightly.

Martin Andersen-Nexö

Peter Glomp. Expectation. 1972

It is certain that the socialist countries are attempting varying solutions concerning the care of the very young child. The aim of all endeavors must be the welfare of mother and child, remembering at the same time economic interests and population policy.

In this context we might mention in passing the question of abortion. There are different views and different ways. In all socialist countries the number of births has decreased in recent years. No doubt, this fact is connected with the growing number of women working and studying. Many who would have liked to have several children now prefer to have one or two only, in view of woman's present dual role. Children are naturally welcome, yet means have been established to give women the chance to interrupt an unwanted pregnancy. The German Democratic Republic set down such rules in 1972. There, as in other countries, objections were raised to the new law, which basically can be reduced to the following:

a)
ethical considerations against interfering with growing life;

b)
fears about increasing immorality;

c)
concern about the outlook for increasing the birth rate.

Since then, the following ideas have crystallized: unwanted pregnancies have always been terminated (in millions of cases in a doubtful way). The question should therefore not be: termination, yes or no? Rather it should be: interruption with the best possible protection of woman's health, yes or no?

It must be stressed that in no country is a woman asked to have her pregnancy terminated. Every woman is left to make her own decision, taking into account ethical and religious considerations.

The decision to have a child is welcome, even though ideal conditions may not yet exist in the family concerned, and generous subsidies are given at birth. This is an expression of the country's desire for more children, but the country wishes to have as many as possible wanted children only.

It is accepted that the possibility of pregnancy termination adds to the freedom of millions of women and increases their happiness, being, in fact, part of their newly won equality.

Fear about an increase of immorality has long since vanished. Women's morals would surely rest on poor foundations if by adopting enlightened legislation a country could be turned into a Sodom and Gomorrah. Termination of pregnancy is not considered an ideal method of family planning. It remains an operation, and negative consequences for woman's health cannot be ruled out. All people concerned are advised to plan their families rather by preventive methods. In the German Democratic Republic, for example, the pill is issued free on a doctor's prescription.

But to come back to the young child: Even though there exist differences of opinion concerning the value of crèches and about the age of infants to be entrusted to them, nurseries are acclaimed everywhere and without reservations. They are one of the best-loved achievements of socialism. In the Soviet Union 13.5 million children of pre-school age attend nurseries and crèches, and the new five-year

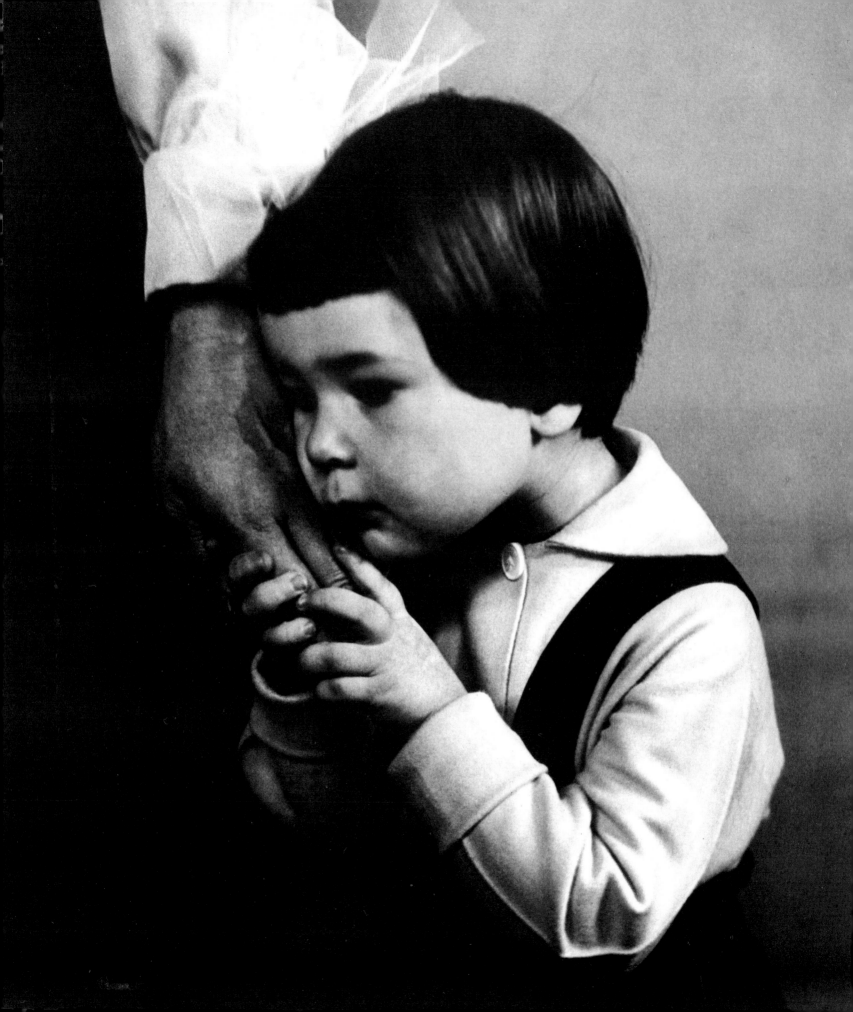

May there always be sun,
And the sky,
And Mother
And I myself.

From a Soviet children's song

Vassily Sumarev.
My house. 1970

Collective work of pupils
from the Heinrich-Heine Schoo
in Hennigsdorf.
Dance under the Peace Tree.
1971

plan seeks to increase this number by a further 2 million places. Bulgaria aims at meeting the entire demand for children's day nurseries by 1980. By the end of 1975, 76% of all Bulgarian children aged between three and seven will be accommodated in nurseries. In 1948 there existed in Bulgaria 99 crèches, but there were 1,016 by 1970. There are now 11,500 nurseries in Rumania, attended by 591,000 children. In 1971–72 alone 21,100 new places were created. Poland plans at present to supply 90,000 more places for children to play and learn in. In ten years places in nurseries in Czechoslovakia have doubled, reaching nearly 500,000. In the German Democratic Republic 68 out of 100 children of appropriate age can find a place in a nursery. A five-year plan will increase the number of places to raise the proportion to 75 children out of 100. In contrast, the countries of the West are carefully planning for a 30% coverage only, with politicians not considering the numbers of children of pre-school age who should attend nurseries, but basing their plans on the estimated demand made by parents.

Behind the statistics from socialist countries there are considerable efforts and expenditure for the benefit of children and their parents. Costs for creating a place in a crèche or a nursery are high for society as a whole, but small for the child's parents. In the Soviet Union the costs for a child in a crèche are 440 roubles a year. Of this the state pays 360 roubles, about 82%, with the proportion for nursery costs being similar. The socialist countries aim, with growing wealth, to assume the entire cost of child care. There is, of course, no pressure on parents to send their children to a nursery. They can, if they wish, bring them up in the traditional way at home. But the quality of the institutions in the socialist countries is so good, and their influence on the general development of children so marked, that a child of suitable age who does not go to a nursery is nowadays felt to be at a disadvantage. In line with sound educational practice, nurseries allow children to learn while playing, and play while learning, and they have an assured place in the general educational

Evgeny Sidorkin. Lullaby. 1964

Corina Beiu Anghelula.
The new home. 1959

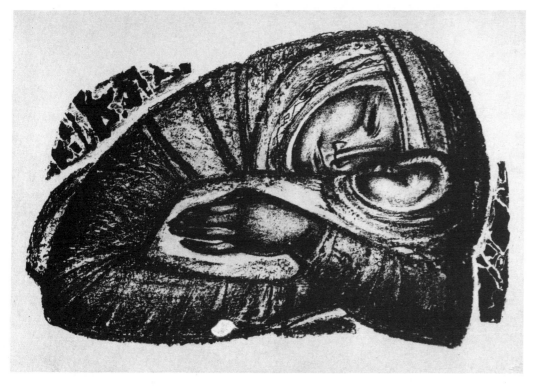

it is again necessary to forget old ideas about man's and woman's place in life. So far the greatest share of looking after children rests on the woman's shoulders. Yet these children are as much the father's, and equality of the sexes demands that both partners share the joys and sorrows of child-rearing. This is laid down in the laws concerning the family in socialist countries. It was Clara Zetkin who pointed to the fact that man's participation in the bringing up of children was not necessary only for lessening woman's burden; it was equally so for satisfactory results in the education of children.

"No man," Clara Zetkin maintained, "should have the superior and misplaced idea that his children are to be brought up in his house by his wife."(38)

And much has been achieved in the rethinking of traditional roles when numbers of women and mothers can work continuously and keep learning while their husbands take it as understood that they share household tasks and care of the children equally.

system. It is therefore not astonishing that the supply of places in nurseries—quickly as this is growing—cannot yet meet the big demand. The need for them has been fully accepted but there are not yet enough. For many women this still means an unwanted long interruption of their career, an interruption which often means not only stagnating but regressing. There are already great efforts in industry to help working mothers. These women are included, if they so desire, in training programs and allowed to take part in the problems of the work collective till such time as they are able to return to their place of work. Because of insufficient child care, socialist industry still loses part of an urgently needed labor force.

This fact and the welfare of children who need educating and getting used to living in a community remain the driving force behind the will to create more and more crèches and nurseries.

For older schoolchildren with working parents, too, all-day child care is a desirable aim. There are many different initiatives under way at present, from circles in children's organizations to working and playing rooms in residential areas, and organized neighborhood help. Working mothers are not left alone to solve their problems. Instead the whole of society takes account of them and will solve them step by step, grudging neither thought nor expense.

To reach a definite solution of the problem

The Second Shift

Another and equally important condition for women to make full use of their equality is freedom from the slavery of housework. There is no doubt in the minds of most women and sociologists as well that the main obstacle to woman's attainment of full stature in the family, her career and public life, is her heavy burden of wasteful household chores, demanding a maximum of strength for a minimum of effectiveness. Here are hidden the greatest reserves for woman's leisure, and this truth did not have to be discovered by today's socialists. Marx made clear in *Capital* that in a socialist society women should be productive outside the domestic sphere, so creating a higher form of family life and relationship of the sexes. (39) In a letter to Gertrud Gaillaume-Schack in 1885, Engels wrote: "True equality of man and woman can become reality only, I believe, when for both of them exploitation by capital has ended, and domestic work is changed into a public industry." Lenin, too, spoke about this problem of equality in many of his writings and speeches, most pointedly in his book, *The Great Initiative.* After remarking that not a single democratic party, nor any advanced republic in the world, had done even "a hundredth part" concerning the equality of women of what had been done in the very first year of Soviet rule, he wrote these words which have become famous: "Woman continues to be a domestic slave in spite of all the laws for her liberation, for she is stifled, suffocated, dulled and degraded by all the petty household tasks, tying her to kitchen and nursery, making her waste her energy in truly barbaric, unproductive, petty, enervating, humdrum and depressing labor. The true liberation of woman and true communism will only come with a massive struggle of the proletariat against the slavery of domestic work, or more clearly, the transformation of it into a socialist industry." (40)

Some socialist countries have done extensive research into the amount of work necessary in the home. In the Soviet Union an enormous number of hours is spent annually in housework, equal to the annual labor budget of nearly 40 million people. In the German Democratic Republic the amount of housework equals the work of some 6 million full-time workers. This heavy burden is carried mainly by "the weaker sex"—a concept still correct as far as bodily strength is concerned.

In a survey among women workers in Leningrad it was found that 81.5% of those questioned did the main part of their housework themselves, 21.6% had no help, 46.2% a little, and 24.3% much help from members of the family.

When the Institute for Market Research in the German Democratic Republic did some research concerning the family schedule, it was found that in about 1,900 households on an average, housework took some 47.1 hours per week. Of this, women did 37.1 hours (more than 80%), husbands 6.1 hours, grown-up children, the grandmother or other helpers 3.9 hours.

As we have seen, with housework to do over and above a job, women are still severely handicapped compared to men. This is expressed in less leisure time. But it dampens also the zeal for work and studying and the readiness to take leading positions, even with adequate qualifications; worst of all it wastes precious talent.

Knowing the facts, how then can there be a solution to the conflict between equality and domestic slavery? A true solution is not achieved by the husband assuming half of the burden to do justice to his wife.

An interesting statement by sociologists in all socialist countries is that there exists a relation between the general cultural level of a man and his willingness to cooperate in the household and the bringing up of children. Men with a better education and higher training are generally more ready to help their wives. This may lead one to think that with a steadily rising level of education woman's equality in the family sphere will become more real. One reason why men are willing in theory to help but fail to do so in everyday life is that they have been brought up in the traditional male role while young, and the results are still noticeable. These men simply are not able to clean, wash or cook, and their wives accept the situation with a sigh. Also, many women lack the patience necessary to tolerate men's perhaps slightly clumsy first attempts at participation, and therefore prefer to do things themselves. Women and men must overcome the remnants of traditional thinking in predestined roles. It is important that things change completely with the young, and that boys receive a training which makes them as fit as girls to do housework.

With such training becoming more and more popular, sociologists should obtain a better analysis of the family work situation within ten or fifteen years. The forging ahead of mechanization of individual household work in socialist countries supplies at high cost only limited relief for women working outside the home. A genuine solution can be reached only if most domestic work can be done outside the home. "The task of economic development should be therefore to extend in quality and quantity those services that meet the needs of the household, and make them into a highly developed branch of modern industry." (41) This is a prime condition for the equality of the sexes, an expensive process which will become reality only gradually. Meanwhile everything possible will have to be done to ease domestic duties for the woman.

It is a great help to millions of working women if the whole family can eat a decent and reasonable meal once a day away from home. Parents may do so at their place of work, and children at school, nursery or crèche. In the socialist countries this is largely taken for granted, and in many households cooking is done only at weekends.

Theo Balden. Mother and child. 1960

Modern, easily cared-for homes are another benefit. The socialist countries build at a great rate, so that every year many people can move to new homes. In the Soviet Union, for example, from 1971 to 1975 fourteen million new homes were completed. In the last ten years half the Soviet Union's population has been rehoused in modern homes. It is worth remembering that 1,710 Soviet towns and worker's settlements and 70,000 villages were destroyed in the war. Homes in the Soviet Union are rented, and tenants do not pay anything towards the cost of construction. Rents are very low, the highest being 16.5 kopecks per square meter of space. Rent is paid only for living space, and not for bath, kitchen, etc. Rents are stable, and empty houses nobody can afford to live in, the raising of rents, arbitrary evictions and discrimination against large families when al-

lotting houses are completely unknown in this as in all other socialist countries.

Many families, in order to "save mother", decide that she should work part-time only. This, however, leads in many cases to the woman sacrificing her career opportunities, or at least limiting them to a large extent in order to allow the rest of her family to be spared dull domestic chores. When, due to health, family or other good reasons, part-time work is woman's only chance to work at all, it can be a valuable solution. However, it is not a panacea, as it limits woman's development and is contrary to equal rights and equal duties in the family. It can hardly be stressed often enough that sharing the "slavery" is very necessary for the time being, with each member of the family encouraged to play a part in running the home. No force, legal or other-

wise, can, of course, be brought to the problem. However, general opinion today, even among most men, tends towards achieving an equal distribution of domestic duties and the raising of children, no longer using the excuse that these are strictly a woman's job.

Indeed many, particularly young families, practice the new division of labor, especially when young couples have seen their own parents working before them.

To halve woman's work at home, "the second shift", is not just a matter of righting a wrong, not exploiting one partner for the greater comfort of the other, much bigger issues are involved. The creative power of millions of human beings must be freed to allow them to live a fuller life. Socialism recognizes this problem, and will in time create conditions to overcome it.

Two, rowing
in a boat,
one knows
the stars,
and the other
the storms.
And one will guide
the boat by the stars,
and the other
through the storms.
And in the end,
the very end,
the ocean will be blue
in the memory.

Reiner Kunze

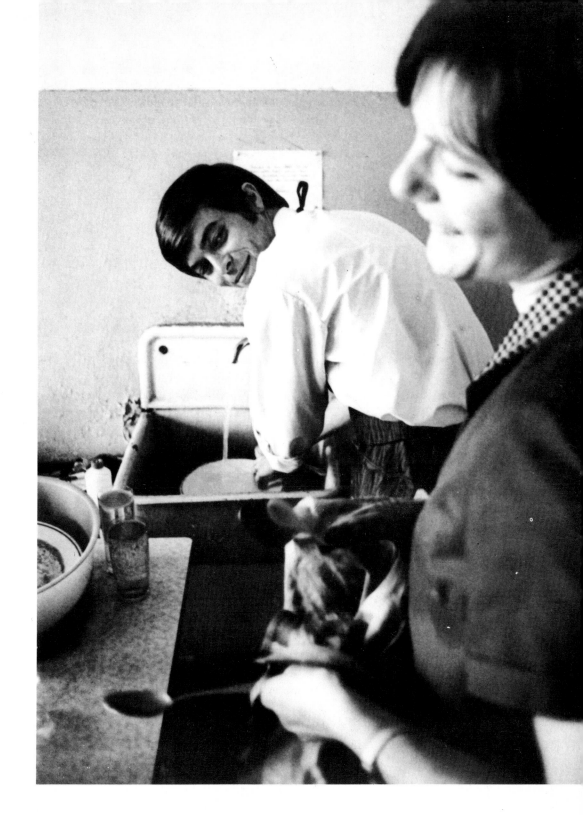

Woman, Socialism, Beauty and Love

Looking through the illustrations of this book, we find represented woman's beauty, woman's love, woman in marriage and family, and again and again love. This, of course, is due to the eternal desire of artists to represent feminine beauty and love, qualities most important in the life of modern women as they were in the lives of their sisters long ago.

As we have said already, it is a misconception to believe that independence, enthusiasm for a career and political activity are contrary to the feminine image. Because of this misconception tourists are often amazed at the charm of Moscow's young women, at the grace and elegance of the women of Prague, the Polish woman's traditional attractiveness, the charm of the Hungarians, and the proud beauty of the Balkan women, not to forget the chic of the Leipzig woman.

Beauty and attractiveness do play their part in the life of socialist women as much as anywhere else. The cosmetics industry is highly developed, supplying first-class products without the need for raucous publicity. More and more beauty salons have been started during the last ten years or so, and they are well frequented. A Moscow cosmetic institute counts women drivers, workers, typists, nurses, dairy-maids, architects, and very many teachers among its clients. The woman doctor in charge of the institute—many surgeons and dermatologists work in these places—said that for teachers it is particularly important to be attractive. She then told the story of a village teacher who received a potted plant from her pupils on International Women's Day. They thanked her for what she was doing, assuring her of her pupils' affection. "But," they said, ,,do go to Moscow, Anna Andreeva, and have your nose made more beautiful." "And," explained the doctor, "being a good teacher, she did."

All cosmetic treatment in the institutes is done on the basis of thorough examination and counselling, and is carefully undertaken and controlled. Treatment includes complicated operations but is not expensive, so that any woman can afford it without difficulties. These treatments are not yet generally available, and further substantial expense is needed together with the training of a great number of experts. All over the world, and in the socialist countries too, care of one's natural assets has become more important when choosing a partner. Of a man an old proverb says: "Man and bear, the uglier, the better"; woman, however, most men desire to be beautiful. Hence the seventeen-year-old Natasha spends as much time in front of a mirror before a date as does her British, French or American counterpart. Even older women are not indifferent to their appearance, and this is as it should be, provided that a woman has more to offer than just a pretty face.

Love, too, is universal, and makes the world go round. Bebel has foreseen that the remnants of prudery are fast disappearing, and young people's relationships are more natural and uninhibited. (42) In the socialist countries, as elsewhere, it is acknowledged that the sexual drive is an important factor of life, but it is not allowed to become all-important, nor made the object of cheap exploitation.

Lenin, in a conversation with Clara Zetkin, discussed this very question: "Communism," he said, "should not mean asceticism but should bring joy and strength to life through a satisfying love life as much as anything else." But Lenin stood against overemphasis, fashionable even at his time, on all matters concerning sex. "I am suspicious," he said, "of those who are constantly absorbed in the question of sex, the way an Indian saint is absorbed in contemplation of his navel ... Even if that sort of thinking gives itself a wild and revolutionary air, it is in the final analysis bourgeois. It is a hobby of intellectuals and circles close to them. It has no place among the fighting class-conscious proletariat." (43)

The naturalness and inner freedom of the young generation is already a result of coeducation in crèche, nursery, school and career training. It is a result also of the self-confidence of young women acquired through equality.

In choosing a partner the young socialist does not consider solely attractiveness and ability. There is an increasing awareness in the young generation that partners should look at life in the same way. Customs, of course, die hard, and the proud girls driving huge combines, parachuting from the sky, or dealing with the problems of theoretical physics, still wait—as their grandmothers did—for a man to ask them to dance. In some countries where equality before the law has become reality, it still is not considered proper for a woman to go into a restaurant without a male escort. Only seldom will a young woman propose marriage, even though she is dying to do

Günter Brendel. Family. 1966

so. In socialist society these are minor matters, no longer taken very seriously, and many anecdotes circulate which illustrate the ways of thought of different generations of women.

Here is one from Tadzhikstan:

"Try this preserve," said the lady of the house. "My daughter, Lola, has made it from plums."

"Take some of these biscuits," said the grandmother. "My good granddaughter, Lola, has baked them."

The guest, a young man called Nasim, thanked everybody politely. But he wasn't all that interested in the miracles of cookery. He looked at Lola tenderly. He loved her.

When the pilaf was served, he was told that it too had been prepared by Lola. Surely the girl had many gifts. She could bake delicious things, embroider wall hangings as beautiful as the starry sky, make pretty dresses, and tiny roosters from melted sugar which the children loved.

"She can do anything," said the lady of the house. "In the whole of Dushanbe there is not another one like her."

Nasim blushed, and Lola bit her lips in embarrassment, even though all that was said was true.

The two were in love with each other anyhow, and they were married soon after. At their marriage feast the tale was brought up in every toast.

They have now been husband and wife for a couple of years, yet—in spite of Lola's gifts—they eat in the factory canteen or in a restaurant, they buy their wall hangings and Lola's dresses ready-made, and get advice about household matters from a service depot. (44)

In another context we have mentioned Bebel's image of woman being as free in her choice of a partner as man, with marriage founded on nothing but affection.

And his vision has become reality. It would perhaps be too optimistic to say that love even now is the only reason for marriage in the socialist countries, but perhaps it is the most frequent and typical one. It would be hard to find a young man who selects his future wife on the basis of what financial advantages she might bring him. Likewise not many young women will marry an unloved man for the security he has to offer. The Polish writer Krystina Wrochno wrote that in the countryside too, love marriage has taken the place of marriage by "acres of land". (45) All this is, of course, obvious when one considers the new concepts of property inherent in socialism.

Rarer even than women marrying for money are women who prostitute themselves. In the socialist countries prostitution as a social phenomenon has ceased to exist. In his book, *The Origin of the Family, Private Property and the State*, Engels wrote: "With the transfer of the means of production to state ownership... there will also disappear the need for a statistically calculable number of women to sell themselves for money ..."(46)

Reality has confirmed Engels's vision.

We have seen previously how woman's position in society was closely linked to the concept of private property.

An argument still used sometimes to keep women out of leading positions maintains that they are "emotional", letting their decisions more often than not be influenced by emotions rather than reason.

Does this argument hold good?

It is no doubt true that some women let their emotions run away with them more easily than men do, thus impairing their objectivity. But this is by no means typical, nor a mystical ingredient of woman's personality. Maybe it was brought about through centuries of special upbringing when emotionalism seemed an inseparable part of woman's psyche. To be clinging, sensitive, able to love and to suffer, were model virtues dinned into women for centuries. If, apart from emotions, a woman was possessed of objectivity and a quick intelligence, she was well advised to hide these qualities, a line of behavior suggested to her in a medieval didactic poem. The so-called feminine virtues were a mockery to millions of women who had to break their narrow limits and go out to work to keep their families alive.

Many of these women who helped to make history in the socialist women's movement neither could nor would be merely "feminine" and emotional. They developed courage, determination, objectivity and strength of will, the very virtues usually ascribed to the male. They brought up their daughters accordingly, and with only few did this mean a loss of pleasing femininity. In the western world, too, most women have completely discarded the outmoded feminine image.

Betty Friedan's book, *The Feminine Mystique*, has been widely read. It is a strong, extremely well-written protest against the artificial restrictions on woman which forced her to seek fulfillment only in the domestic arena, concentrating solely on husband and child to the complete exclusion of an outside world which is constantly growing more interesting. The upbringing of little girls, says Betty Friedan, frequently still directs them towards one aim only: marriage. Their whole imagination is channelled towards one focus: a marvelous wedding day, followed by happiness ever after. This dream, conjured up a hundred times every day, is bound to lead to eventual disappointment in the humdrum reality of woman's daily routine. Helga Hörz in her book, *Die Frau als Persönlichkeit* (Woman as a Personality), also points out that stressing the emotional tendencies of women means forgetting the historical character of these artificially bred qualities. She also maintains that some men may have emotions as intense or even more so than woman. "If we look at women," she says, "whose social circumstances have dulled all their feelings or even killed them, the whole absurdity of schematically assigning certain qualities to the sexes becomes clear. There are also many women who in their objectivity and their emotions are superior to many men. If one were to ascertain the differences between the sexes, it would be necessary to create approximately the same living conditions as well as provide both sexes with equal education and training."(47)

Socialism has met these conditions to a large extent. Since liberation from fascism a new generation has grown up which shows clearly that the enormous social changes of these years have created and are still creating a change in the human psyche. The idea that being emotional is feminine and being objective is masculine has long since been questioned by a new generation. When here and there it is used as an argument against placing a woman in a managerial position, this is merely a vestige of the past, and no longer an opinion held by many.

All the same socialism, as indeed any other system, agrees that men and women though equal, are not the same. Their physical roles are different, and so are their physical qualities. Women have a weaker skeleton, they are smaller, with a lower and broader pelvis, and a more delicate formation of tissue and skin. Women tire more easily, and only have 60 to 70 per cent of man's strength. Essential psychological differences concerning character and will-power can, however, not be proved scientifically. In the literature on the subject a few special psychological qualities, considered specific to the sexes, are described, and they must obviously be acknowledged. Women are said to be more easily hurt, they are more impressionable, with a keener sense of adaptation, and a marked need for contact.

These traits are often used as an argument against women, again when it comes to placing them in leading positions. But everyday experience shows that these very qualities if matched with ability and knowledge can make most excellent managers.

There are also people who warn that women might be in danger of losing their precious feminine qualities by taking on too much responsibility. These people's anxiety makes them blind to reality. There are many in the socialist countries who can quote examples proving the contrary. The female town mayor has grown closer and closer to the community, year after year, very personally involved with its welfare. There is the chairman of an agricultural collective, energetically fighting for its greater prosperity, yet in the course of debate ready to throw into the scales not only arguments but her feminine charm. Some Soviet professors at the international center for nuclear research at Dubna might tell the following tale: When the young and very gifted mathematician Natalya Shirikova defended her thesis before a board of famous scientists, after a few hours, and with a little apologetic smile, she asked for a short break. "The twins," she said, "you will understand, they must now be fed."

It is certain that the desirable and pleasant differences between the sexes are stressed, too, under socialism, and people who were worried about women's special qualities being lost in the years of hard struggle will now be at ease. In fact, there are today many more interesting women who have all the attributes of feminine charm.

Heinz Kahlau, a disciple of Brecht, made this discovery for himself, and expressed it in a poem in 1964:

The Other Sex

Of young women I should like to say
To smile, to ask, they have a way,
The way our vanities they bear,
No man could ever match.

These women's love is of a kind
That drives us on to greater things in space.
A debt to them and us we owe.
And yet they kiss us as we go.

It would be nice if women young and clever,
Who in themselves do trust
And later in us trust as well,
Could finish works men have begun,
Yet keep their smile—kind as before.

Günter Glombitza. Young couple. 1970
Christo Stefanov. Spring in old Plovdiv. 1965

Inge Götze. Tapestry

TENDERNESS

To do something
for oneself and for others
all at one time.
The finest of tendernesses,
enriching.

Love, divided into
loving and being loved,
always ready for either.
Taking in that way
is giving.

Proving to oneself
and to others
that to be human
is wonderful.
Or else
we shall stand
in our chains
helpless and naked.

Heinz Kahlau

Fritz Cremer. Young love. 1961

WHAT I WANT

I want to know all weathers,
see a genuine Titian,
invent a computer,
and understand at last
what "beautiful" does mean.

Dieter Schnappauf

Love and respect and confidence speak from these lines, but perhaps also the tiniest bit of worry. "It would be nice..."

Some ten years have passed since the poem was written, and women have amply shown that they can combine ability with smiling kindness.

Women in turn enjoy qualities many men have newly acquired: special attentiveness, richer feelings, friendship and solidarity. These are a valuable extra to that "male attraction", just as good and as difficult to define as feminine charm.

Equality may even increase this charm, and if some women lost it in the struggle to get ahead, it was the lack of equality that made them hard. In the future both sexes are bound to develop their qualities naturally.

Another point, often discussed, is that under socialism woman took a stand against monogamous marriage. It is true that in the far-reaching changes of a revolution all values, including marriage, were questioned. Engels called it "a strange fact that with every great revolutionary movement the question of "free love" takes priority with some people; this is considered revolutionary progress, a throwing off of old, no longer necessary traditional fetters; with others it presents a welcome doctrine, providing a comfortable cover for all kinds of unrestrained relationships between men and women."(48) As mentioned in another context, after the victory of the October Revolution there were quite a few adherents of "free love", some outstanding socialist women temporarily among them, such as Alexandra

Kollontai. Lenin considered these phenomena to be an exaggeration which could be explained by the enormous upheaval in which all ideological values lost their binding power. "New values then crystallize slowly and with difficulty. This includes human relationships—relations between man and woman when emotions and thought are revolutionized."(49) The idea for a pamphlet, *Freedom in Love*, came to Ines Armand, a well-known Bolshevik, before the revolution. In letters to her, Lenin discussed this plan in detail. He declared that the call for "free love" met, in the final analysis, not a revolutionary but a bourgeois demand. The general public would understand it as freedom from seriousness in love, from

having children, from marriage, even if Ines Armand had intended it to stand for better things. (50)

For a short time some revolutionaries in the Soviet Union took a negative view of marriage, and many thought that marriages could be dissolved as quickly as they were entered into. But in the end the conviction prevailed that through the achievement of equality marriage had taken on a completely new quality, and man and woman could find in it something no "free love" can provide in the long run: security, for children too, mutual assistance and responsibility, and true partnership.

Discussions in the Soviet Union eventually brought clarity to the question, as it did in the

communist and workers' parties, so that the revolutionary changes in other socialist countries gave rise to few theories of "free love" and rejection of marriage. On the contrary, marriage has become again, and perhaps even more so, a desirable institution. More than 6,000 marriages are celebrated every day in the Soviet Union. And there will be a great many more in all socialist countries, where the state helps young couples start their life together with many special privileges, for example, long-term interest-free loans.

Faithfulness is by no means considered old-fashioned by today's youth. During a discussion on the subject for readers of a women's magazine in the German Democratic Republic, it became clear that the concept of loyalty is now interpreted much more broadly. "Loyalty," it was said, "is much more than not being estranged. It is to stick together in good times and bad, to help one another to progress, to be there when the partner is in need, stick to him even if he sometimes disappoints or makes mistakes that cause others to doubt him. That is loyalty." (51)

The modern idea of marriage differs perhaps from what is meant by "modern" in non-socialist countries. It should certainly mean living with each other on the basis of equality.

It is only natural that problems remain. The greatest love can often cause the greatest pain, and marriages do come to grief. The number of divorces is higher than it was before liberation from fascism. Of every ten marriages an average of two are unsuccessful, but this is, of course, no argument against marriage under socialism or any other form of society.

In many divorces woman's new self-confidence is expressed in the fact that, independent through a career of her own, she will not endure the yoke of an unhappy marriage. The divorce rate for recent marriages, up to about the fifth year, is rising steeply in some socialist countries, while divorces of marriages of eight years and longer are fewer. Marriages need time to stabilize, and many young people do not give their marriages a chance to do just that. It is in some ways positive and progressive that they should not take things as unchangeable. On the other hand many part too easily without even trying to maintain their marriage.

Every socialist country faces the task of preparing their young people for marriage better than they have done so far. They need education for love much more than sex education, which can only be a part, and not even the most important, of the general education for love. The emotions need developing, the ability for friendship, consideration and a sense of responsibility. Children should be instilled with high ideals, high standards in the choice of a partner. The close coordination of home, school and youth organizations should create an attitude towards the opposite sex which mobilizes the best qualities in boys and girls.

The better the preparation for love and marriage, the more real equality of the sexes becomes in all spheres, and the more outmoded traditions and concepts give way, the stabler and happier will be the marriage of the future.

Woman in socialist society ... she has not yet achieved all her aims, but she is well on the way, well on the way to full realization.

Quickly they have sheltered
under the maple tree.
But its leafy roof is not thick
enough against cloudbursts.
Then the two took his coat
to shield them:

the girl stands, her shoulder
leaning against his chest . . .
A car passes on its way to town,
the driver smiles: the two still stand
though it's stopped raining
long ago.   Stepan Stshipatshov

There is nothing more beautiful
than walking with you through the fields
at dusk, when the tranquil green meadow
is full of what has been.
Day is within us,
yet night is drawing closer,

like the sound
of your voice.
Kurt Steiniger

Notes

References are to the German publications, used by the author. Quotations in the text are rendered freely by the translators.

(1) **Engels, F.,** Der Ursprung der Familie, des Privateigentums und des Staates. Bücherei des Marxismus-Leninismus, Vol. 11. p. 57

(2) **Bebel, A.,** Die Frau und der Sozialismus. Berlin 1964. p. 58

(3) ibid. p. 58f.

(4) **Zetkin, C.,** Zur Geschichte der proletarischen Frauenbewegung Deutschlands. Berlin 1958. p. 207

(5) **Marx/Engels,** Manifest der Kommunistischen Partei. Berlin 1945. p. 21

(6) **Bebel,** op. cit. p. 35

(7) **Zetkin,** op. cit. p. 77

(8) The International was founded in London in 1864. It brought together workers' associations beyond national frontiers, on the basis of Marxism which it strongly defended against all kinds of reformatory disturbances.

(9) Proudhonism—named after Pierre Joseph Proudhon (1809—1865), a noted French socialist and forerunner of anarchism—was an opportunist movement among the French working class.

(10) In Britain and France several unions for women were founded, partly because outmoded prejudice kept women out of men's unions, but also because the women in these unions were engaged in particularly feminine occupations. To begin with these unions fought for better working conditions, without declared political aims.

(11) **Zetkin,** op. cit. p. 89

(12) ibid. p. 89

(13) ibid. p. 111

(14) ibid. p. 111

(15) ibid. p. 114f.

(16) ibid. p. 124f.

(17) **Bebel,** op. cit. pp. 3—4

(18) **Bebel, A.,** Die Frau und der Sozialismus. Stuttgart 1895. p. 14 (This paragraph was abridged in later editions.)

(19) **Bebel,** op. cit. p. 515

(20) Die Gleichheit. 14. 2. 1910

(21) The pamphlet, "Die Krise in der Sozialdemokratie", is referred to.

(22) **Zetkin,** op. cit. p. 147

(23) In the pursuit of this idea Lenin kept in mind a well-known statement by Karl Marx: "Anyone who knows anything about history, also knows that great social changes cannot be achieved without the ferment provided by women. Social progress can be measured exactly by the position of woman in a society . . ." From: Briefe an Ludwig Kugelmann, Marx/Engels, Werke, Vol. 32. Berlin 1965. p. 582f.

(24) **Lenin, V. I.,** Werke, Vol. 30. p. 100 (in Russian)

(25) Turkestan included the present Soviet republics of Turkmenia, Uzbekistan, Kirghizia, Tadzhikstan and the south of the Kazakh S.S.R.

(26) The traditional garment was the *parandzha*, enveloping woman from head to foot.

(27) **Lenin, V. I.,** An das Büro des Frauenkongresses des Petrograder Gouvernements am 10. 1. 1920, in: Werke, Vol. 30. Berlin 1961. p. 289

(28) Proletkult is an abridgement for *Proletarische Kultur*. It was a movement of the radical Left in the arts of the twenties, rejecting all cultural achievements of the past.

(29) In 1866 Karl Marx wrote: "What I mean by education are three things: first: intellectual education, second: physical training, third: polytechnical training which will provide an understanding of the general principles of the production process, at the same time introducing the child or young person to the practical use and handling of the basic tools in many kinds of work." Marx/Engels über Erziehung und Bildung. Berlin 1966. p. 164

(30) In all socialist countries the aim is a ten-class *Oberschule*, as it exists already in the German Democratic Republic.

(31) Sozialstatistik der "Europäischen Gemeinschaft". 1971

(32) **Marx/Engels,** Die deutsche Ideologie. Werke, Vol. 3. Berlin 1959. p. 74

(33) **Marx, K.,** Zur Kritik der Nationalökonomie, Ökonomisch-philosophische Manuskripte. Bücherei des Marxismus-Leninismus. Berlin 1955. p. 101

(34) **Chartschew (Khart'iev), A. G.** and **S. I. Golod,** Berufstätige Frau und Familie. Schriftenreihe "Soziologie". Berlin 1972. p. 125ff.

(35) **Reding, J.,** Natascha liest auf Rolltreppen, in: Zu Gast bei Freunden. ed. Peter Schütt. Dortmund 1972. p. 34

(36) **Chartschew,** op. cit. p. 158

(37) **Urlanis, B.,** Die Formel des Glücks, in: Sowjetunion, No. 7 (280). Moscow 1973. p. 46

(38) **Zetkin, C.,** Über die sozialistische Erziehung in der Familie (1906), in: Die Erziehung der Kinder in der proletarischen Familie. Berlin 1960. p. 42

(39) **Engels, F.,** Herrn Eugen Dührings Umwälzung der Wissenschaft. Marx/Engels, Werke, Vol. 20. Berlin 1962. p. 296

(40) **Lenin, V. I.,** Die grosse Initiative. Werke, Vol. 29. Berlin 1959. p. 418f.

(41) **Chartschew,** op. cit. p. 159

(42) **Bebel,** op. cit. p. 516

(43) **Zetkin, C.,** Erinnerungen an Lenin, in: Ausgewählte Reden und Schriften, Vol. III. Berlin 1960. p. 129ff.

(44) This tale was written by Borchon Crani, and is quoted from: Sowjetunion, No. 10 (283). Moscow 1973

(45) **Wrochno, K.,** Die Frau in der Volksrepublik Polen. Warsaw 1969. p. 69

(46) **Engels,** op. cit. p. 81

(47) **Hörz, H.,** Die Frau als Persönlichkeit. Berlin 1968. p. 94

(48) **Engels, F.,** Das Buch der Offenbarung, in: Marx/Engels, Werke, Vol. 21. Berlin 1962. p. 10.

(49) **Zetkin, C.,** Erinnerungen . . . op. cit. p. 129ff.

(50) **Lenin, V. I.,** Brief an Ines Armand, in: Briefe, Vol. 4. Berlin 1967. p. 49f.

(51) **Für Dich.** Illustrierte Zeitschrift für die Frau, No. 11/1973. p. 4

(52) **Kuba,** Gedicht vom Menschen. Berlin 1950

Bibliography

Ansorg, L. Kinder im Ehekonflikt, in: "Elternhaus und Schule". Berlin 1968

Aralowets, N. D. Die Arbeit der Frau in der Industrie der UdSSR. Berlin 1956

Bardensheuer, R. Woher und Wohin. Leipzig 1918

Beauvoir, S. de Das andere Geschlecht. Hamburg 1951

Bebel, A. Aus meinem Leben, parts 1—3. Stuttgart 1910—1914
Die Frau und der Sozialismus. Berlin 1964
(ed) Die Jugendgeschichte einer Arbeiterin, von ihr selbst erzählt. Munich 1909
Über die gegenwärtige und künftige Stellung der Frau, in: Glossen zu Yves Guyot's und Sigismonda Lacroix's "Die wahre Gestalt des Christentums", 3rd edition. Berlin 1892

Borrmann, R. Jugend und Liebe. Leipzig, Berlin, Jena 1966

Braun, L. Die Frauenfrage. Leipzig 1901
Frauenfrage und Sozialdemokratie. Berlin 1896

Dohm, H. Der Frauen Natur und Recht. Berlin 1893

Dornemann, L. Clara Zetkin—Leben und Wirken. Berlin 1973

Engels, F. Der Ursprung der Familie, des Privateigentums und des Staates. Bücherei des Marxismus-Leninismus, Vol. 11. Berlin 1950
Die Lage der arbeitenden Klasse in England, in: Marx/Engels, Werke, Vol. 2. Berlin 1957

Fornalska, M. Erinnerungen einer Mutter. Berlin 1968

Frauen der Revolution. Porträts hervorragender Bolschewikinnen (from the Russian). Berlin 1960

Frauen im Spiegel der Kunst (Group of authors). Leipzig 1972

Die Frau in der Volksrepublik Bulgarien. Sofia 1959

Frauen in der Tschechoslowakei (ed. Czechoslovak Women's Committee). Prague 1963

Geschichte der deutschen Arbeiterbewegung, Vols. 1/2. Berlin 1966

Die Geschichte der Frauenbewegung in den Kulturländern. Handbuch der Frauenbewegung in 3 Teilen. Berlin 1901

Geschichte der Kommunistischen Partei der Sowjetunion. Berlin 1960

Grandke, A. and **H. Kuhrig** Das neue Familiengesetzbuch der DDR, in: "Einheit", No. 11. Berlin 1965

Grandke, A., Misgeld, G. and **R. Walther** Unsere Familie. Leipzig 1973

Hieblinger, I. Frauen in unserem Staat. Berlin 1962

Hörz, H. Die Frau als Persönlichkeit, in: "Unser Weltbild", Vol. 53. Berlin 1968

Jesper, K.-H. Frau und Religion. Leipzig 1959
Die Töchter des neuen Bulgarien 1944—1964. (ed. Bulgarian Women's Committee)

Key, E. Florence Nightingale und Berta von Suttner. Zurich 1919

Kollontai, A. M. Wege der Liebe. Berlin 1925

Khart'iev, A. G. and **S. Y. Golod** Berufstätige Frau und Familie, in: "Soziologie". Berlin 1972

Kuczynski, J. Studien zur Geschichte der Lage der Arbeiterin in Deutschland von 1700 bis zur Gegenwart. Berlin 1963

Kultur in unserer Zeit. Zur Theorie und Praxis der sozialistischen Kulturrevolution in der DDR. Berlin 1965

Kurella, A. Das Eigene und das Fremde. Berlin, Weimar 1968

Lenin, V. I. An das Büro des Frauenkongresses des Petrograder Gouvernements, am 10. 1. 1920. Werke, Vol. 30. Berlin 1961
An die Arbeiterinnen, am 11. 2. 1922. Werke, Vol. 30. Berlin 1961
Die grosse Initiative. Werke, Vol. 29. Berlin 1959
Die Sowjetmacht und die Lage der Frau. Werke, Vol. 38. Berlin 1961
Rede auf dem I. Gesamtrussischen Arbeiterkongress am 19. 11. 1918. Werke, Vol. 28. Berlin 1959
Über die Aufgaben der proletarischen Frauenbewegung in der Sowjetrepublik. Rede auf der IV. Konferenz parteiloser Arbeiterinnen der Stadt Moskau am 23. 9. 1919. Werke, Vol. 30. Berlin 1961
Über die Losung der "Entwaffnung". Werke, Vol. 23. Berlin 1960
Werden die Bolschewiki die Staatsmacht behaupten? Werke, Vol. 26. Berlin 1961

Luxemburg, R. Briefe aus dem Gefängnis. Berlin 1946
Die Krise der Sozialdemokratie (Junius-Broschüre). Ausgew. Reden und Schriften, Vol. I. Berlin 1951
Frauenwahlrecht und Klassenkampf. Ausgew. Reden und Schriften, Vol. II. Berlin 1951

Marx, K. Briefe an Ludwig Kugelmann, 12. 10. 1868, in: Marx/Engels, Werke, Vol. 32. Berlin 1965
Der Bürgerkrieg in Frankreich. Berlin 1952

Marx, K. and **F. Engels** Manifest der Kommunistischen Partei. Werke, Vol. 4. Berlin 1959

Mehring, F. Geschichte der deutschen Sozialdemokratie, Vol. III. Berlin n.d.

Michel, L. Buch vom Bagno. Memoiren einer Kommunardin. Berlin 1962

Mileva, L. Der tapfere Zug. Sofia 1972

Miller, R. Vom Werden des sozialistischen Menschen. Berlin 1960

Moral und Gesellschaft. Entwicklungsprobleme der sozialistischen Moral in der DDR (Group of authors). Berlin 1968

Neubert, R. Das neue Ehebuch. Rudolstadt 1957
Die Geschlechterfrage. Rudolstadt 1956

Neumann, I. Die Frauen der Französischen Revolution. Quellenhefte zum Frauenleben in der Geschichte, 14. Berlin 1927

Nogina, O. P. Mutter- und Kinderschutz in der UdSSR. Moscow 1950

Oglobin, I. Berufsausbildung in der UdSSR. Moscow n.d.

Pieck, W. Clara Zetkin—Leben und Kampf. Berlin 1948

Pohlmeyer, H. Um die Befreiung der Frau. Berlin 1955

Polte, W. v. d. Unsere Ehe. Leipzig 1968

Popova, N. Die Gleichberechtigung der Frau. Ihre Stellung in der Sowjetunion. Berlin 1948

Probleme der Frauenqualifizierung (ed. Herta Kuhrig), in: "Soziologie". Berlin 1971

Reicke, I. Die Frauenbewegung, ein geschichtlicher Überblick. Leipzig 1929

Schirrmacher, K. Die politische Frauenbewegung in Frankreich und Deutschland. Berlin 1906
Die Suffragettes. Weimar 1912

Staatliche Dokumente zur Förderung der Frau in der Deutschen Demokratischen Republik (zusammengest. u. bearb. v. U. Adomeit). Berlin 1973

Suttner, B. v. Lebenserinnerungen. Berlin 1969

Thönessen Frauenemanzipation, Politik und Literatur der deutschen Sozialdemokratie zur Frauenbewegung 1863—1933. Frankfurt on the Main 1969

Thoms, L. and **E. Kohn** Bebel und die Frau der neuen Zeit. Berlin 1962

Thorndike, A. and **A.** Das russische Wunder. Berlin 1963

Um eine ganze Epoche voraus (ed. Arbeitsgemeinschaft "Geschichte des Kampfes der deutschen Arbeiterklasse um die Befreiung der Frau", Päd. Inst. Leipzig). Leipzig 1970

Vom Auftrag zur Wirklichkeit. Vom ersten zum zweiten Frauenkongress der DDR (ed. Bundesvorstand des Demokratischen Frauenbundes Deutschlands). Berlin 1968

Weltkongress der Frauen Kopenhagen, Juni 1953 (ed. IDFF). Berlin 1953

Wer zählt die Völker Brockhaus-Autoren berichten über die UdSSR. Leipzig 1972

Wrochno, K. Die Frau in der Volksrepublik Polen. Warsaw 1969

Zetkin, C. Erinnerungen an Lenin. Ausgew. Reden und Schriften, Vol. III. Berlin 1960
Ich will dort kämpfen, wo das Leben ist. Auswahl von Reden und Schriften. Berlin 1955
Zur Geschichte der proletarischen Frauenbewegung. Berlin 1958

Zetkin, C., Duncker, K. and I. Borchardt Die Erziehung der Kinder in der proletarischen Familie. Berlin 1960

Zu Gast bei Freunden, in: Kleine Rote Reihe 12 (ed. P. Schütt). Dortmund 1972

Recommended Reading:

Bebel, A. Woman in the Past, Present and Future. London 1885

Engels, F. The Origin of the family, private property and the State. London 1972

Lenin, V. I. Works. 12 vols. London 1936/38

Marx, K. Capital. 2 vols. London 1887

The poems on the pages 48, 89, 114, 139, 145, 155, 180, 207, 210 and 211 have been abridged.

Illustrations